the Gallery
SHARON DEESE

The Gallery

This book is written to provide information and motivation to readers. Its purpose is not to render any type of psychological, legal, or professional advice of any kind. The content is the sole opinion and expression of the author, and not necessarily that of the publisher.

Copyright © 2020 by Sharon Deese

All rights reserved. No part of this book may be reproduced, transmitted, or distributed in any form by any means, including, but not limited to, recording, photocopying, or taking screenshots of parts of the book, without prior written permission from the author or the publisher. Brief quotations for noncommercial purposes, such as book reviews, permitted by Fair Use of the U.S. Copyright Law, are allowed without written permissions, as long as such quotations do not cause damage to the book's commercial value. For permissions, write to the publisher, whose address is stated below.

Printed in the United States of America.

ISBN 978-1-951913-73-1 (Paperback)
ISBN 978-1-951913-74-8 (Digital)

Lettra Press books may be ordered through booksellers or by contacting:

Lettra Press LLC
30 N Gould St. Suite 4753
Sheridan, WY 82801, USA
1 307-200-3414 | info@lettrapress.com
www.lettrapress.com

This book is dedicated to two very special men.
Mr. L. S saved my life more than once.
And
Mr. S. S was always there when I needed a friend.
I LOVE YOU BOTH WITH ALL MY HEART
I pray to GOD to watch over them, keep them safe.
To bring them love and happiness while
Going on their way.
GOD BLESS YOU

I will love you always

Contents

Poems
By S.D. Vojtko

A Friend 9
Always and Forever 10
Always Loved 12
Angels 13
Awaking 14
Bonds 15
Christmas Eve 16
Forever Now 17
I Heard Him Calling 18
I'm never going to be 19
Life's Prize 21
My Sweet Savior 22
Never alone my friend 23
Spring 24
Staceyo 25
Tell the world 26
The Book 26
The Call 28
The Lake 29
The only man for me 30
The sweetest man I ever knew 31
Things you need in life 32
We have each other 33
When I found love 34
Your Love 36
Yours 37

Contributing Author
Poems by
Robert T. Ware

After Dawn 41
In The Moment 42
My Blue Angel 44
My Struggle 45
Roses Are All Red 47
Sixteen Things 48
Star Light 50
Storms of Life 51
The one for me 53
Worse than Death 54

Short Stories
By SD. Vojtko

A New Beginning 57
Big Sister 66
Carol 72
Fred 77
Lee's One Stop 90
My Early Years 102
My Start in Life 124
Our lives go on 135
Peppy and I 145
The Winter Snow 150
Three Little Words 153
Without You 157

Poems

By S.D. Vojtko

A Friend

Have you ever wondered where a friend came from?
Or how it all began?
Have you ever held a hand of someone or washed
Away the tears that sadness brings?
Was forgiveness ever given, from one to the other?
Was there a time when laughter sounded just like thunder?
Did you romp in the sun, or play in the rain?
Enjoying life as one?
Did you see things as they really were?
And encourage each other to be strong?
Was there a time when you were all alone?
And no one with a hand for you to hold?
For in a moment you can lose someone and life will never be the same.
A friend is someone you can trust will always be there for you.
Someone for caring and sharing all you happiness, joys and pain.
Someone that listens without given blame.
Who will wipe away the tears of sadness,
and walk with you in the rain.
All this I learned through you my friends.
this is how it all began and
I'm so proud to call you my friend.

Always and Forever

We were young and so in love.
I knew we were to be as one.
She said she wanted to be my wife.
We made plans, hopes of happy days
and for bright tomorrows.

Then one day she looked at me and said,
I can't I can't be your wife.
I can't live with you and your life.
I have to be me, be myself.

I loved her so, my heart was broken.
She was my tomorrow my forever more.
She walked away without saying good-by.
She walked away like she didn't care.
Always and forever wasn't there.

Then she was gone, the pain was so bad
I wanted to die.
But God said "My son you must go on,
There are many important things you need
to get done. You will see life goes on."

MY heart turned cold, I would do my job.
I studied hard, and did go far.
I knew hard work was the only way.
I keep friends and family far away.

My cold, cold heart was here to stay.
As I lost my loved ones, my heart grew colder.
Always and forever was not for me.

I didn't have time to open my heart,
not to the hurt and the pain that was within.
Not to a love that could have been.

I did my job and I did it well,
I had no one to care or to be proud.
No one to talk to, no one to tell.
Always and forever was not for me.

As the years go by, I think of the people
I met on the way, a few that care
and wanted to stay. Some got to close
and I pushed them away. I said mean
things and walked away.

I was afraid to let down my guard, I didn't
want the pain, I didn't want them to know
| did cared too. What would people say?
Who would really care what would they do?
Always and forever was not for me.

Now time has passed by,
I hope someone would care. I have no one to
talk to no one is there..
No one to call my own, no one to love,
no special friend.

Is this what I want till the end?
Always and forever alone without a friend.
GOD PLEASE HELP ME WHAT HAVE I DONE.
Always and forever alone, with no one to care.

Always Loved

I know that you still doubt it
You don't want to hear the words.
Just know one thing as you go about your life.
You will always be loved.
In your darkest hours and lonely days
If your jogging in the park or walking in the rain.
Somewhere out there a friend is calling your name.
Some people show their love with pride with no shame.
Love is patient and kind it fills your heart with joy.
It's not aggressive, jealous or rude,
not always right or wrong.
Love can and will bear all things it will never fail.
Love is guaranteed to put a smile on your face,
A spring in your step as you stroll along.
All love asks of you is to be true to yourself and others.
How do I know this because as long as I live my friend,
You will always have someone that cares for you till the end.
You will always be loved.

Angels

Have you ever wondered where Angels came from?
Do you know who they really are?
Have you seen them before at another time or place?
They seemed to know all about you what you need and face.
When they put their arms around
you can you feel their grace?
There are times that I have problems that I cannot solve
and I ask GOD to help me before I fail.
As I sit all alone just talking to GOD I feel the warmth of a
loved one from up above. I know it's
an Angel I can feel the grace.
Somehow my Angel has opened a door and I fear no more.
Yes I believe in Angels and know who they are.
They are the loved ones that's left us
GOD sends from heaven above,
to help us fine peace, happiness and love.
Never be afraid to ask them for help
GOD is always there to open
HIS arms and fill you with His Love and Grace.

Awaking

Awaking with the morning sun,
I reach out to the bright new day.
To glorify, magnify the wonders
of the world you made.

Early in the morning I will seek your face.
Seeing love in all the things you've done.
Hearing the birds sing, and the flowers all
the bloom the smells are so becoming they
bring me so much joy.

Thank you for the colors you've giving me
so much beauty.
I see peace, joy and love in all the things you do.
Yes Load, I thank you for your son too.

Dear Lord I know you are so great.
Oh Heavenly Father, I love you so.
But that is something you already know.

Bonds

Upon thinking of time and space.
I know of the heart to heart bond.
Or the love a mother has for her son.
Families have troubles and tears flow.
With you and your friends there is a bond too.
With hope, joy and dreams for all to see.
Between you and me we make a bond too
Something very special it grow and grow…
And often just like strangers, we drifted apart.
But we will always have a bind in our hearts.
Once a bond is made it is hard to be broken.
Some were deep inside there is a speck of hope.
That someday that bond will burst wide open.
For the joy of our bond will never fully be broken.

Christmas Eve

The night before Christmas I sat all alone.
Waiting to see is Santa would come to my home.
The snow was falling lightly blowing all around;
my fireplace was going with a crackly sound.
As I sat here looking at my Christmas tree standing in
the window for all to see, all green, gold and white.
With star on top shining so bright.
On the door was my wreath with its bright red bow.
A few reindeer on the lawn lite up the snow.
Santa and his elves were playing too.
Frosty was out there waving his arms for you.
The lights outside with their pretty colors reminded
me of the past when there was just you and me.
I never thought I would be alone on Christmas Eve.
The fire started dying and soon would be out, so I drank
the last of my wine turned off the TV, the rest of the
lights would stay on for the eve. As I said my prayers
I thanked God for this year I may be alone but in
my heart you are near.
Merry Christmas Dear Jesus, Happy Birthday too.
Someday soon I'll celebrate with you.
As I crawled into bed I was sure I heard the
tiny little feet of eight little reindeer.

Forever now

You did the calling to our Father's side.
You've done the drying to be our guide.
Of all the tears I cried you helped me hear
the knocking at my door.
In this heart you will dwell for ever more.
You've always been here at my side.
Helping me to abide, even at life's troubled shore.
In this heart you will dwell for ever more.
oh sweet Jesus to me,
You are my Comforter, forevermore.
Now help me to honor
to uplift and magnify
Our Father and His only Son.
In this heart you will dwell forever more…

I heard Him Calling

I can feel the sunshine upon my face.
I can feel myself floating on a gentle breeze.
I can't feel any pain I am totally at easy.
I can hear a voice calling, calling me back home.
I know the voice I'm hearing is coming from above.
As I look around I see the ground moving farther away.
I see people crying, others that are praying,
They all knew that I couldn't stay.
Now I hear the Angels singing the clouds have opened up.
They are standing there waiting the Gate is open wide.
I hear a voice calling Welcome Home my sweet child,
You've been away so long.
Now I have my white robe, a halo and wings.
Yes I'm home again and as happy as I can be.

I'm never going to be

I'm never going to be the women you want me to be.
I'm never going to run or jog around the lake with thee.
I'm never going be as pretty as the women that you see.
I'm never going to be slim, trim and happy and gay.
Or swaying to the music in some man's arms.
I'm never going to be healthy, younger, wealthy or wise.
But for some people that's all they can see with their eyes.
All I'm ever going to be is just plain
me, always just the way I'm.

Were I've been is a long lonely road,
with no one to really care.
All I was is just someone to lighting their load.
I was only good as a help hand or to
care for them till the end.
Someone to take their burdens off their hands.
I've been used and abused with no one to care.
This was my cross to bear.
My life has been so lonely filled with despair.
No one to listen no one to really care.

There was a young man once that I loved with all my heart.
But our years was far apart, he couldn't
understand friendship.
You could see the companion the car-
ing he had in his heart.
He had been hurt so much before he didn't understand.
That my type of love for him was for a very special friend.

Why are people so afraid of love? There so much more.
You can love someone with all your
heart but only as a friend.

A couple of times I almost died, he stood by my side.
He fought so hard to keep me alive.
I asked God why I had to stay.
Why did He make me feel this way?
He told me, (your work for me is still not done.)
Just believe in Me with all your heart
try to endure the pain.
Things never stay the same sometimes, things can change.

I'm never going to be the women of your dreams, just me.
But I hope you'll understand I'll always
think of you as a friend.
I will care for you, will pray every day until the end for you.
But the love I have for you will always
be deep within my heart.

Life's Prize

Hey you there with the smile in your eyes,
What do you think is life's greatest prize?
Do you think it's a huge balloon?
Or do you think it's a trip to the moon?
Maybe you feel it's the leaves on the trees,
Or could it be an autumn breeze?
Did you see the birds up in the sky?
Or did you see the butterfly?

Most of life is beautiful to see,
These are things that mean a lot to me.
Let's take a look at life's reality,
Its greatest prize is still very free.
It's a thing that we know as Love,

Hey you there with the smile in your eyes,
What do you think is life's greatest prize?
Do you think it's a trip to the snow?
Or do you think it's a big rainbow?
Maybe you feel it's the animals you see,
Or could it be a bumblebee?

Did you see the moon in the sky?
Or did you see the clouds drift by?
Is this life feel like a zoo?
Does it hold a place for you?
Have you searched over hill and vale?

And seek these things on Love's own trail?
All these things God has made in the world.
Hey you there with the smile in your eyes,
What do you think is life's greatest prize?

My Sweet Savior

In the pitter patter of my mind,
Love is growing, you will find.
Even in sorrow and feeling low.
I've been down that darkened road,
Fell so often beneath the load.
He found the light within my soul.
Jesus my Sweet Savior lifted me.
I had not the will to live,
And nothing more to give,
Now I have eternity,
For in Him I am free.
Can I share Him with you?
Jesus my Sweet Savior will lift you too.

Never Alone my friend

You will never stand lonely
You will always have a friend.

I see the tears in your eyes
I understand the sorrow in your heart.
I've been through it time and time again
And if you need, I'm here to be your friend.

You will never stand lonely
Jesus, He came to be my friend.
A bond between Him and me
He alone knows our hearts

All the time call upon His Name
He will fill your heart
Erase all the pain.
You will be filled to overflowing
All your life will be The Light glowing.
Never alone, We always will have a friend.

Spring

I looked into my heart today
To see if I could find a reason
To be happy a place all mine
A meadow where the birds
Sing brightly and the butterflies
Float by on a gentle wind blowing.
Were all the pretty flowers blooming?
And the bees are everywhere.
I can see all the animals come out to play.
I see peace and all the glory that Love can
Sometimes bring. I feel the sunshine on
My face and know it is Spring.

Staceyo

Staceyo, Oh Staceyo why must you go?
I'm off with my Pop to England and Rome.
Don't worry my darling someday I'll come home.
Staceyo, Staceyo the man of every woman's dreams.
Eyes as bright as diamond's hair as black as coal.
His smile leaves broken hearts everywhere he goes
He has left them in Spain, London, Paris and Rome.
He made an appearance in Paris this spring.
All the young ladies wanted church bells to ring.
But right now for him that is not the thing.

He must move on there is so much to do.
The places his seen the things he has done.
Like have a picnic while watching the rising sun.
His Pop keeps him moving, there's work to be done.
Work always comes first my son,
Then off to town to party, when it's all done.
Staceyo, Staceyo I miss you so.
Don't worry my darling soon I'll come home.

Tell the world

Tell the world about our Lord,
tell about him now.
Did you see someone sad and alone today?
And told them God loved them.
Have you told someone that God Cares?
And wants to do great things in their lives.

Did you tell of His Love and the things He can do.
Have you taking the time to thank Him yourself,
For the wonders he has done in your life.
Have you thanked Him for his love, your life?
Family and friends.
Do you show that his love is true and all
He wants is what is best for me and you.

The Book

As He checks the Book
Will He find your name?
Will He walk by you?
and there will Him remain.
Come to the Lord,
and you, He will not betray.
As you take Him for your Savior,
He will cleanse your heart too.
Then you will be whole again.
With a brand new start waiting
for you.
You belong to Him and He belongs
to you,

The call

Little bitty rain drops falling on my head
Early in the morning raised me out of bed.
I feel the rain drops falling, I hear the wind
Roaring, that's calling me back home.
I see the leaves that are brown covering
the earth all around.
I hear the wind roaring hat's calling me
back home.
The birds singing reminding me
of the songs we used to sing.
Why did I stay away so long?
I hear the wind roaring.
That's calling me back home.
Soon I will be in heaven where I belong.

The Lake

I sat at the lake watching the rain,
My heart was broken I could feel the pain.
When out of nowhere, this gentleman came.
He sat down beside me looked into my eyes,
He called me by name.

As he took my hand the stars started to shine.
He said see you have no reason the cry.
We walked and talked about the past, and now.
He told me how precious and special I was to him.
Because you see he loved me before, loves me
Now and will forever.

No matter what is said, for people can be mean.
Just follow your heart and live your dreams.
I will always be with you, whenever you need me.
As the sun started to rise, my heart filled with joy,
I smiled at him and said.
Thank you Lord for holding my hand, for walking
with me I now understand.
Thank you for loving me just the way I am.

The only man for me

Oh how do I love him, will he ever really know.
My heart is broken, and the pain hurts me so.
But through the pain my love still grows.
It will never run out for this God knows.
What have I done to deserve this pain?
My love for him, he is not to blame.
He gave me hope and a reason to live.
With a smile like sunshine and stars in his eyes.
His loving compaction and understanding care.
I know in my heart He would always be there.
Each time I saw him it grew more and more.
I told him I loved him, all he asked was why?
I told him the truth, I could not lie.
But the years between us were more than a few.
And people you know can always be cruel.
All he could say is I'm sorry good-by.
Soon he was gone and out of my life.
I was alone, heartbroken and unloved again.
But I still know, my love for you darling was true.
Stay safe in God's Arms for this I still pray.
Always listen to him and follow his way.
Thou we are apart, my heart still yours.
You will stay with me always forever more.
Then maybe the Lord will tell me way.
You're the only man I'll love till the day I die.

The Sweetest Man I Ever Knew

I met a man, his eyes were blue.
The sweetest man you ever knew.
He was always around in and out.
Now he loves to fly all about.
This wonderful man is so nice.
You wanted to keep him by your side.
His words were so kind and understanding.
This man that loves unconditionally.
Whenever you really needed a friend
He was always there with a helping hand.
His compaction was soft his feelings were so real.
No truer friend Staceyo will I ever find.
I miss you so much, but I understand were ever
you are; you're in GOD'S loving hands.

Things you need in life

What is important to you in your life?
How is it going is everything alright?
Have you ever wondered how strong you
were? Or were the strength came from?
Until being strong was the only choice
you had If not for yourself but for others.
So what are the things in live do you need,
The first and foremost is Our Lord God.
Then take time to look for something good
in your day. A rainbow the sunshine or A
friend's smile.
Then you will find that you have everything
that you need. Courage, Strength, Wisdom,,
understanding and love for others, these are
some of the things you need.
To take everywhere you go. Always lend a helping
hand a smile to help others on their way.
Then you will know the peace of God everywhere
you go.

We Have Each Other

When I look at you, I see me.
I feel your heart what it longs to be.
I have the freedom that dwell within.
I love the day, and the night time too.
I love to play to work my friend with you.
I have the joy and understanding that all
of who are guided by God's gentle Hand,
I see you stand in loneliness and sorrow,
Come to our Lord His strength we will borrow.
It will last till the end of time?
when I look to you, I see me.
I know in my heart were I longs to be.

When I found Love

As I laid in my bed asking God why,
Why am I still alive, I cried?
My life has no purpose, on one cares.
I had no reason at all to go on.
I asked God if you want me to live,
Give me a sign, someone to care for me,
someone all mine.
As I laid there crying for time passes slowly,
Sleep was just starting when to my surprise
My door opened wide there he was like a
ray of sunshine walked In to my room.
His eyes were like stars, his smile so bright.
My heart stop, I couldn't speak,
I looked in to his eyes.
All I could think was No God not him.
But when He touched me I know it was he.
My heart to him and he would never understand.
I didn't hear a word he said I saw only the
care in his eyes.
They say look in to a person's eyes and you
see their soul. His was like pure gold.
As I lay in bed I asked God Why.
This man is too young, and wasn't for me.
But each day I waited for his voice, his smile.
Each day my heart beat stronger and stronger.
Soon I was home and all alone, I couldn't wait
to see him again.

What would I say, how would he feel?
Oh God help me what do I do? I looked for help
to end this feeling. I was told to tell him how
I felt to tell him the truth.
I wrote him a letter, but had to tell him myself.
This was the hardest call I made in my life.
He was so kind and sweet, he laugh and I weep.
He didn't think someone would believe he was a
Gorgeous, Handsome guy. Or that someone would
love or care for him in his life.
A million time I could say I love you and it would
never be too much.
All my cards or letters were all in vain.
No one call no one cared no one came.
Soon I heard he had moved away.
So much hunt, so much pain.
The one thing I know is that my love for
him is true and pure.
He will stay in my heart forever and always.
God has gave me a love so true, someone that
was the best thing that ever came in to my life.
As I pray each night I as the Lord, please Bless
Him watch over him, keep him safe and from harm.
Please let love shine on him if only in my heart, Amen.
If only we could have talked maybe this would have
had a happy end some were along the way we may
have been friends.

Your Love

I always thought roses were sweet and that the
Rain came to grow them
And then I thought the sun would always shine,
Even behind the clouds.
Then I saw a thousand candles burning, bringing
Promise of light.

But the roses they soon faded, as the sun remains to hide.
All the candles burned away, and
that left me with no light.

But you left me your Love, which
does not fade as the roses.
You left me your love, which outshines the sun.
That does not burn out like a candles promise.

Your Love will out shine any candle, and outlive any rose.
I know it is so true because I was told God loves me.

Yours

Like the Mighty wind I rush in,
To a love that is so divine.
Come with me and you will see
What love was meant to be.
Caring, holding, a gentle kiss, finding
Finding someone, all lives happiness.
Some seek peace some for joy.
But I have something no one can destroy.
I know a true love all my own.
A love that gives me more then I
Will ever know.

Contributing Author

Poems by
Robert T. Ware

After Dawn...

Shackled and chained with a self-imposed brand of shame.
Confounded and bewildered, I struggle
to remember my name.

Searching for a way out of hell, but my eyes are shut tight.
I pray for daybreak just to escape this dreadful night.

A soft but auditable voice reverberates from all around.
"Just wait" "Just wait" while knelt upon the ground.

In the darkness, a brilliant bright beam pierces through.
The expectation of daylight causes
me to take a breath or two.

Hours turned into days that seemed to go by without end.
From out of nowhere, came the call of a welcoming friend.

The words that were spoken set my thoughts free.
Belief that hope, joy, and laughter will soon return to me.

I dedicate this to Tonia thanks for the inspiration.

In a Moment...

Love
Love will enter the room.
Love will fill your heart.
A heart can be filled with love.
A kiss can make time stand still.
a diamond ring will make her cry.
Love will see you in her eyes.
Wedding bells will ring.
Love will dance, for the first time.
Love will never ever leave you.

Happy
A joyful tear will fall.
A warm smile can appear.
Children's laughing will fill the air.
Snow falls gently to the ground.
A hot air balloon is able to race the sun.
A balloon will drift away.
A beautiful baby will be born.
All your troubles can be over.
A smile can brighten your day.

Inspiration
You will know the answer.
The future will become the past.
You will know what you can do, if you try.
A dream can come true.
Mom's hug can ease your fears.
A kiss can make the hurt go away.
A solider can come home.
Time will take these feeling away.

Sad
The music will become silent.
A shining star falls from the sky.
"I love you" will be unspoken.
A bond will be broken.

Bad
Tragedy can come, and life will splinter.
Life can be swept away.

By R. Ward

My Blue Angel,...

The one I hold most high.
Let's see your smile, don't be shy.
With lips so sweet, I long to kiss.
A moment away, it's you I truly miss.
Your eyes like stars taken from the sky.
Take my hand and I will draw you nigh.
A vision of beauty, I wish to behold.
My passion for you, grows so bold.
My love for you could not be more true.
Why are you so down and blue?
Tragedy came like a theft in the night.
Our happiness was stolen and left us fright.
May I dry all of your tears?
Can I chase away your fears?
Sitting motionless in your sorrow.
Waiting helplessly for tomorrow.
I take the blame for the mistakes I made.
I will pay the price until my debt is paid.
With your wedding band of gold.
Why have you turned so cold?
Why have taken your love from me?
Please stay and hear my plea?
Oh how I long for your kiss.
It's you I truly miss.
Don't be blue
I'm sorry for hurting you.
My Blue Angel.

By R. Ward

My Struggle

I sit upon my throne, surveying all with great delight.
Self anointed ruler, I stole all in sight.
I rule over all, who will come and who will go.
In a seasons time, I will reap what I sow.
As each day passes; drawn out like impending doom.
Consumed by darkness, that flows from every room.
Sadness grips me, in its merciless squeeze.
Unrelenting pressure, forcing me to my knees.
What once was happiness, has been replaced with pain.
Shivering and cold, from a hard driving rain.
I struggle for hope, that just escapes my reach.
Happiness still eludes me, and despair is in the breach.
FIRE! FIRE AT WILL!!!, is the battle cry of me and my foe.
As bombs fall around me, I have no-where to go.
My enemy deals in pain, and this I can relate.
Un-aware of their mercilessness, and ignorant of my fate.
Pedaling death and deception, is the nature of this beast.
I dine on paranoia, in a grandiose feast.
I tell myself lies, for I believe they are true.
Hurting those close to me, is what I must do.
I've judged myself and I have found, that I'm without blame.
The love of my life, however I've worked hard to frame.
Confined by these walls, I conspire in their decline.
I've bound us together in a prison, of my own design.
As the morning sun brakes, I can see! I can see!
Satan has tried to deceive, all this time my enemy was me.
I awake from this dream, gasping for my last breath.
To see the lowering of a casket; its my life after death.

May you rest in peace, the pastor said.
While in my shame, I bowed my head.
As soft as I could whisper, oh Lord save me.
Love rallies round, and one…,two…,three…!
Jesus held out his hand, and helped me stand.
With no delay he did say, follow me and I will restore your life and land.
Walk away and your disaster, it will not linger.
Hell will open up, and I will not lift a finger.
I confessed my offenses using rhythm and rhyme.
My hope is in time, forgiveness from my victims will be mine.
If this poetic confession, sounds even remotely true.
Ask the son of God, to enter your heart and save you.

Written By: Robert Ware

Roses Are All Red,...

Roses are all red, and it's well known to be true.
How much greater is my love for you?
As sweet as honey, mixed with morning dew.
As deep as the ocean, beautiful and blue.
As bottomless as the abyss, and timeless as your kiss.
As warm as a hug, on a cool fall day.
As welcome as your touch, when I pass your way.
My love for you has, and will always be new.
If roses they are all red, and violets they are all blue.

Written by: Robert T. Ware

Sixteen Things 1 Corinthians 13

Sixteen things all combined each and every one.
If you can't comprehend it, this might know a ton.
Love is more than a word, to be whispered with a kiss.
In these next few lines, I hope the idea you do not miss.
Love is a verb, an action that's tough to follow.
Jesus did for us, and some find it hard to swallow.
This is the essence of love, in its sensation and surprise.
Be sure to read it all, and don't cover your eyes.
1. If I can speak in a language that all can understand,
and if I do it without love in hand, I'm
just a noisy member of the band.
2. If I possess the reward of foresight and can grasp
all that is hidden from sight and can know all that I might,
if I have all faith that I can make mountains fall,
but if I have no love. I am surely nothing at all.
3. If as my submittal of all that I own
to those whom have little,
and offer my flesh up to the flame, if done
withholding love. Emptiness is mine who should I blame.
4. Love will endure, until the end of time.
Love eases the pain, without spending a dime.
Love wants nothing that others possess.
Love takes no glory, or claims that it's the best.
Love does not desire its own high status of plenty.
5. Love will not leave you exposed and empty.
Love does not pursue, after love at all.
Love will stay peaceful, in a hateful brawl.
Love retains no count, of any wrong thing.
6. Love takes no pleasure, from a hurtful sting.

Love celebrates what is true, and actually there.
7. Love eternally defends those in its care.
Love believes in the admirable, without pause.
Love persistently expects good, lacking cause.
Love relentlessly safeguards, and humbly stands tall.
8. Love in no way stops, and will never stall.
But where there are forecast, it will not last;
where there is speech, it will be silent in the breach;
where there is intellect, it will fall in to neglect.
9. For we only know a fleck and we can barely predict,
10. But when love comes to perfection,
flaws will have no detection.
11. When I was a kid I spoke as a child did,
my thoughts were those of a boy,
my reasoning was more like a toy.
But when I came to be a man,
I sent the foolish ways to a distant land.
12. Now we only see the pitiful image that we reflect;
after this and face to face we shall truly detect.
Now I know in small; then I shall know
it all, even as I am notorious.
13. Faith, hope, and love now these
three remain and are glorious.
But the cream of the crop, the one that rises to the top.
The greatest of these is LOVE.
Love is I'm sure, Gods greatest unconditional prize.
Love is treasured most highly, by the three and the wise.
For God so loved the world and this, I know was no fun.
Out of his love for you and me, he gave up his only son.
Love is a gift to be given, not to be received instead.
So if you looking for love, you've been misled.
If love is not in action, sorrow will persist.
Love has no feelings, and out of
the sixteen no feelings exist.
Written by: Robert Ware

7 Aug. 2010

Star light...

The stars shimmering light.
The stars shinning so bright.
The cluster of stars, I see this night.
I wish that I may, I wish that I might.
Gathers them together, as gift for your delight.

Written by Robert T. Ware
9 November 2011

Storms of Life....

A storm is brewing angrily on the horizon.
It's a vicious squall leaving misery in its wake.
A plague devouring lives, make no mistake.
It carries with it all manner of strife.
Devastating homes and destroying life.
The movements of the clouds are as warships of wrath.
Floating majestically on a pre-determined path.
Clouds are billowing, ominously dark and gray.
The winds start to blow with a roaring grown.
That rises to a infinite and terrifying tone.
A screeching pitch amid the winds swirling round about.
Drowning out every blood curdling scream and futile shout.
Thunder rumbles across a darkened sky.
Accompanied by the Reaper winking his eye.
Lighting flashes that blinds your sight.
Your heart begins to race and fills with fright.
The deafening "CLAP!" of a sonic boom.
Soon there will only be a sorrowful gloom.
The trees are set in motion, as they rock and sway.
Peace in the center of this storm, but it's too dangerous to stay.
Just ahead of this most dreadful gale.
There is a frantic exodus of enormous scale.
The numbers of refugees rise to be great.
There are still so many more that chose to wait.
There are pitfalls and follies for every decision made.
In the finale a tremendous levy will truly be paid.
As if anguish and regret are being pored over our graves.
There isn't a moment that passes while looking at the sky.

That you think to yourself today is a good day to die.
In a back draft of destruction swept up by a cyclone.
Finding ourselves in a cemetery of memories left standing alone.
Wanting to not be here or anywhere, wishing you never existed.
Duped by ignorance each account you've listed.
Clutching sweet dreams made of nightmares.
While sending out Morse code and shooting flares.
Never thinking this storm would last so long.
Wondering what was done and where it all went wrong?
The storm is coming to an end with little ceremony.
The sky is clear and gray clouds have gone away.
Speechless, in the end I don't know what to say.
Written By: Robert T. Ware

The One for Me...

The path to the one for me, has taken many a step.
The search of which, you can't fathom the depth.
There are so many out in the world to see.
Without trying I've found the only one for me.

Dreams came and went, that left me felling blue.
With a touch of her hand, I know this love is true.
There are so many out in the world to see.
Without trying I've found the only one for me.

She has quickly become my friend that's best.
With a love like hers I can forget all the rest.
There are so many out in the world to see.
Without trying I've found the only one for me.

Days turn to weeks and weeks turn into years.
I only hope to fill her life with smiles no more tears.
There are so many out in the world to see.
Without trying I've found the only one for me.

She is the riches of my hearts deepest desire.
My love for her burns like a raging fire.
There are so many out in the world to see.
Without trying I've found the only one for me.

I've longed for her every day of my life.
When I found her, I made her my wife.
There are so many out in the world to see.
Without trying I've found the only one for me.

Written By: Robert T. Ware

Worse than Death

Surrounded by strangers, everything appears unknown.
It looks as if I'm lost, even in my own home.
I'm tormented by crisis, in a doggish persecution.
Minuscule glimmers of hope, that render no resolution.
Sleep eludes me, when I lay down at night.
Sweet dreams slip away, and are replaced with fright.
I'm seized by terror in a quite enjoyable attraction.
All has fallen noiseless, eerie, and void of any action.
I'm crippled by stillness, and in its frozen grip.
I beg for mercy, but merely receive the whip.
Gasping for air, yet swallowing tears.
Mourning the lot, I've lost over the years.
In this gloom, there are tiny shimmers of light.
Out of the frightful darkness, the shine takes my sight.
Praying for death, and frequently meet with despair.
Merciless sorrow, consumes me everywhere.
Tethered to a sense of direction, with no bearing?
I ask for assistance, aide turns up without hearing.
Opinions are only words, and most are freely given.
Blinded by their insanity, the truth is often hidden.
Without much thought, of the impact they've imposed.
Punch drunk and beaten, my flesh is raw and exposed.
I scream the names of my loved ones to come near.
As I wait for their arrival, they are no longer here.
Somehow life has wondered off course, and gone astray.
I imagine that around the bend, will be a new day.

Written by Robert Ware
... _ _ _ ... Have I lost way? ... _ _ _ ...

Short Stories

By SD. Vojtko

A New Beginning

It was Saturday night Jim and I were meeting some friends for Dinner. It was a surprise birthday party for Jim's sister, she will be thirty on Monday. We met at the Hunter's Inn. We were going to give her the over the hill party. There were about fifteen people, friends and family we had a lot of fun. Dinner, dancing and funny gifts. Jim and I gave her a crying towel and gift card. Joan and Paul some wrinkle cream plus a gift card. Mom and dad some black roses. Jim's mom and dad a crying pillow. She received a few other things then Joe her boyfriend gave her a large candy ring. He turned to her with a big smile and said (Meg I love you will you marry me), she said this was to big to wear to work, but yes I will marry you. With that he pulled out a little black box and said would this be better, Meg started crying oh yes. We all had a toast with champagne to their engagement.

Most of us started leaving around 11:30. It was along ride home. Joe's and Meg parents were in the van, they had to start planning a wedding. So Meg and Joe rode with us. We were talking about the wedding and making a list of who would be asked to stand up for them. Then the guest list when out of no were headlights were coming at us. We had nowhere to go we were on a bridge, the van was hit and then hit the brick wall, and two other cars started sliding and spinning and one hit us. Then one hit the car behind us. After all stopped I could hear yelling, screaming and a baby cry, I black out.

The next thing I knew was that the lights were bright and people talking. One of them sounded like our friend Joan, a man was telling her that the people in the van didn't make it. One person in Jim's car didn't make it, two were hurt one with a broken arm. He couldn't say names till next of kin were called. Joan called Joe's uncle and Jim's aunt they were on the way to the hospital. The people in the car behind us were hurt be not bad the baby was fine. Four cars were drag racing down route 419 and at the speed they were going couldn't stop. Two drivers were dead, one hurt bad in hospital one in jail. I blacked out again.

I half woke to sounds I knew I was in the hospital. I couldn't move or open my eyes. I heard people talking not ever word but some. I knew I was badly hurt every time I would start to wake someone would come in and I went to sleep. Sometimes I could hear the doctor talking or touching me but couldn't move or talk. I don't know how long this went on until one day I heard Kathy, Kathy the doctor was calling my name but I couldn't answer. The doctor told the nurse my heart beat went up so they could decrease on the pain meds. To call him if something happened. I fell back to sleep.

One morning a nurse came in and said Morning Kathy it's time for your bath. I opened my eyes a little and said okay. She turned and smiled saying she would be right back. She returned with an aid and said doctor Bales was on his way. He came in with a big smile and said welcome back, he checked me out and asked how I felt. Told him not to good, head hurt, my neck hurt a lot, so did my legs. He said your head hit the side window, a dice in my neck had to be replaced, my right side was bruised, my legs were pushed under the dash and I had to be cut out of the car. I would be okay in time and with physical therapy. The police wanted to see me but he would have them wait a few more days. Did I have any questions? Yes who died in our car? He looked at me I said I know everyone in the van died, the car behind us were fine. But who died in our car? The nurse took my good hand and he said Jim died. I started to cry and asked to see Joan. And thank you for telling me I was tired now and wanted to rest he nodded to the nurse and she put something in my IV and I went to sleep.

When I woke Meg was there with Joe, I was so happy to see them and they were alright. I asked how long I was in the hospital, over five weeks. I missed the funerals. That Joe moved into his folk's house and Meg moved back to her folk's home. We talked about the funerals. Joe's parents were buried on Monday and Meg's parents and Jim on Wednesday. I asked if anyone from my side were there and she said my two uncles and one aunt came. They came to see me at the hospital but were told I was being kept out because of the pain. Uncle Roy went to the office with Meg and signed over power of attorney to her, they called him after the accident to treat me he is the oldest relative I had and he is 1400 miles away. Meg would keep him and the family updated as we go along. I was happy to hear that. They even helped Meg and Joe pack up my apartment and move my things over to Meg's till I knew what I wanted to do. I was to stay with her when I got out and was ready to be on my own. We laughed and cried and soon I was tired so they were going to leave and would be back tomorrow. That evening the doctor came in and took off the neck brace that felt great, I had to be careful for the next few days but coming along nicely. He said the police would be here in the morning after breakfast and would I like someone in the room with me, I said no.

I did sleep well that night. Breakfast came and I asked to sit in the chair, so they helped me get into it. No one showed up so for lunch my legs were hurting so I was put back into bed. I just had lunch and my pain medicine when two officers came in. I was sleepy and they said they would come back, I said do it now get it over with. Said they only had a few questions and would leave, Okay let get it over. They asked my name, date of birth and address. Then what did I remember about that night? I told them about the party and leaving for home. We were talking about the people to invite when out of no were and a lot of lights were coming at us. We were on a bridge and no place to go. The van was hit first and pushed into the wall, there was two cars sliding and one hit us head on. The other one hit the car behind us and after it all stopped I could hear people screaming and yelling then a baby crying. I must have blacked out. Nothing till I woke up in the hospital.

They asked a few more yes and no questions then told me about the accident. Four boys were drag racing down route 419, two died one was in hospital and one in jail. The people in the van didn't make it, the car behind us were okay they were on their way to the air force base in the next town so the base send a truck for them and their things. Joe and Meg were taking to the hospital first, Jim and I had to be cut out of the car. Jim didn't make it. I started to cry and the nurse can in and said it was time to leave doctors' orders. Said I needed my rest they said good bye and hopped I would have a speedy recover, I thanked the nurse and she gave my something for pain.

I missed dinner but woke when Joe and Meg got there. Joe went to get me a salad and Meg was telling me about her talk with the doctor that afternoon. I would start physical therapy in a few days, when I could start walking I would have to walk up to a hundred feet and back to my room before he would think of letting me go home. It would take a while but I will do it, I would have to use a walker to start but not always. That was fine with me sounded good I would be able to get out of bed. Joe came back with my salad said he hopped it was okay he had to make it and not sure what I liked. I told him it looked very good, so I ate it all just for him. They stayed till eight we talked about how they were fixing my bedroom, they were putting me in the master room because of the shower and how close the bathroom was for me to get to. Meg took over her old room. I thanked her and she went to get me a soda from the machine, Joe thanked me for not arguing with her she, just couldn't sleep in parent's room. I told him I had that feeling it was okay,

The next three days went the same, one day the doctor said that Jeff would be in the next day to start my therapy. He would give me a list of things I could do on my own in bed or in my chair, I was still to have a nurse help me up. I told Meg that night what he said, that I was glad to get started. Now that Joe's arm was better he was back working so would only be here on week-ends. That gave us time to start talking about the wedding. Wedding colors, bridesmaids she asked me to be Maid of honor, people to invite and invitation's, what kind and how many. The cake was going to be made by her friend's mother, she had worked in a bakery for many years and that was her gift to the kids. Nice that is one of the big tag items. She sat up my computer and printer in the den so we could look a cards and invitations, she had been taking pictures of flowers and dresses with color charts from the stores she been going too. We will be well on our way when I get home, yes I started calling it home.

6:30 Monday morning Jeff came in so we could get started. He said the first few days was just working my muscles in both legs, I have been off them now for two months and couldn't stand or start walking. He did each leg for 20 Minutes and asked if I had someone that would help me at night to move them up and down and bend them, I didn't have the strength to do it myself. He would be back tonight to do it and if someone would help then he would show them how. Told him I would call Meg but she works till four and can't be here before 4:30. He would make me his last treatment for the day. Meg was here when he came it, He showed her how to hold the foot and turn the ankle, next push the foot up so the knee and hip was like this. While I was in bed every once in a while I was to try and do this on my own, but not to push it I would know when to stop. Try 15 to 20 minutes every four hours. We said okay when will I be up walking? When he felt my legs would hold me on my own with the walker. Maybe a week may be less.

For five days we did the bed, then on the sixth Jeff gave me my walker and said now we stand, He helped me up and we just stood there for a few minutes. Then he had me bend my legs, not taking steps just bend. Okay now we will walk to the door and back. Lean on the walker that is what you have it for. We did it twice then back in bed and he rubbed my legs. Told me Meg and I could do this tonight but with a nurse and only what we just did no more. We did this for two days, have to go slow don't want a setback. He said by Monday we would start trying the hall, ten to fifteen steps at a time. I shouldn't wait to tell Meg, she has been a big help. On the week-ends Joe would help.

Monday I was up and ready when Jeff arrived, we start slow and I made it to the hall he keep asking how did I feel? Then he showed me the mark on the wall and said I could do this tonight with my friend then turn back and rest. He left Meg the orders for her. She was over joyed when she read them, before you know it you will be doing your two hundred. We did this for two days, Jeff said every two days we would add more steps. By the end of six day we were up to fifty feet one way. I want to cry. That was one hundred round trip. By day ten up to seventy five feet, one hundred forty round trip. Twice a day was fine I wanted to know when I could go out on my own, not as far but some with the walker. Next week, Monday we did one hundred one way, but instead of turning we keep walking all the wing back to my room. Jeff said that was the same as turning around. He told Meg we could do the same at night. I could take the walker and do up to the fifty feet mark on my own a few times a day but not to let myself feel pain or we would have to slow down. I was to tell the nurse so they would chart it and watch for me. I would do it at 10:30 and at 1:30 after lunch. Then with Meg at seven and nine before bed.

Monday Dr. Bales came in he had a big smile, he read my chart and said I was doing fine he was sending me to have tests and ex-rays to see how things on the inside were doing, if all was better I would go home next week. This time I had a big smile, he wanted to watch my head. The swelling was gone, he just wanted to be sure the clod was gone too. My neck and legs looked well just try not to fall and hit my head. As soon as Meg got there we started making plans for me to leave. I was to ask if it could be a Saturday or Sunday so Joe could help me at the house. So when I saw the doctor he said that would be fine to make plans for this Saturday. Yes I have been here for three and a half months and was ready to leave, there was no rehab in our town so here is where you stay till you're ready for home. Told Meg Saturday was the big day so she started taking things home and would bring a box every day and pack things for me. As I looked around I could see all the stuff family and friends gave or sent to me. Told Meg good idea or we would need a truck to do it in one trip.

Joe and Meg were there at ten but I had to wait till two for my discharge papers, and my list of drugs to get and my appointment to see the doctor. It was so nice to get outside, the weather was nice the air smelled so fresh and clean. I asked Joe if we could let down my back window. When we arrived home Joe helped into the house there is a gravel walkway and he didn't want the walker getting stuck. I was taken to my bedroom and Meg helped my change. They had all my stuff put up so I could see them. Told her soon we would have Joe bring some boxes up from the basement and we would have a yard sale. I was tired so laid down Meg would get me up for dinner. It was nice to set at a table and eat with people. We talked about my rules till I went to see the doctor, a home care nurse would be by tree days a week to help me shower and shampoo my hair. Meg was still working so this was a good idea. I would be home most of the day by myself, was to use the walker till doctor said, I could go into the den and work on my computer and if I got tried was to lay down. She would may my lunch when she made her and leave it in the refrigerator.

Two weeks later we went to see Dr. Bales he was happy on how well I looked and walking, around the house I didn't need the walker but if I went out I still needed it. The way people on the streets move all over and don't watch were they go it would be better for a while. It would be a long time before I could drive that was fine Jim and I only have one car and I'm not ready to get a new one. We ate dinner out and we updated

Joe on how the appointment went. When we got to the car we started talking about old times and I was getting upset so was Meg. Then Joe said okay that is the pass we will never forget the ones we lost, but they would want us to move on not live in the past. Let's remember the last time we were all in the same room, all the fun we were having and nothing more than that. We knew he was right and life goes on.

Joe said we have a wedding to plan, Meg laughed we have been working on that while Kathy was in the hospital. So we updated him on that and I told them I have some things printed out to show them and would fill in the dates as soon as they found a church and a hall. That they had to do. So as of today we will miss the ones that left us, but get on with our lives that is what they would want. We knew Joe was right and told him so. After we looked at the invitations and R.S.V.P. cards they decided on the one I liked. Joe left at ten and Meg helped me to bed. She told me the nurse would be here in the morning at ten, soon I would be up and jogging with her I sure hope so. She also asked if I would stay with her after I was well. I could stay as long as I wanted or at less till the wedding I was up to me but please think about it. She needed me as much as I needed her, we were like sisters even thought I wasn't married to Jim. I was to her for life. Told her not to tell Joe that he may change his mind. She laughed she already did and he was okay. They haven't set a date yet so I told her it was fine with me, that when I could work again it will give me time to build up a savings but I wanted to help with food and bills. Meg went to bed happy and as I laid there I told God that I was glad for all the good things and people He put in my life, and He was right each day is a new beginning.

Big Sister

I've been a member of the Big Brother Big Sister program now for 2 years. I've been paired up with some pretty sad girls. Some stay in the program to see if they get things they wanted, or if you will give them money. But I had two girls that really wanted the friendship and help I could give them.

Carolyn was a sweet girl, she was 11 had no dad, but 4 older brothers. 1 was married Fred and his wife lived in the next town over. Mom was gone a lot and Carolyn had to do things around the house and the cooking. I started picking her up once a week from school. We would go to the park and get her homework done then out for dinner.

After a few weeks I was able to bring her to my house. We started with Wednesdays then Saturday too. We always did the homework first then went out or played games. Talked a lot and as she started telling me things, I was the one to start worrying. I talked to my supervisor and wrote in Carolyn's file things she said. Family life wasn't going well. Soon she was staying overnight or 3 to 4 days with me. On day her mom called to say Carolyn was in the hospital. She was hurt and would I go to her. Mom was too busy.

When I got to the hospital the police were there. She was beat up and raped. Carolyn said she didn't know who he was only she was home alone when he came in the back door. She didn't want to talk about it anymore. Mom told police I was to be given temporary custody so I would be taking her home.

Officer Roberts told me it was ok, just be sure I let my boss know. I called Jane before we left the hospital two days later.

About a week later the police were at my door, the DNA was back and they needed to talk with Carolyn. We sat in the front room and I stayed with her. Turned out mom's boyfriend came over drunk, the police picked him up that day. Mom didn't know it was him but was so mad at Carolyn. She was going to turn her over to DCFS. That is where Fred and his wife stepped in. They have gone to court to have Carolyn placed in their care. Mom is ok with that so she will be leaving as soon as school out for the summer. So for 5 weeks I had Carolyn Monday till Friday, then Fred or Mary would pick her up Friday night and bring her back on Sunday night.

I was so happy to see the change in her. She had nice clothes, smiling all the time and her grades went up she was passing to the next grade. The last day of school Fred, Mary, mom and the boys were all coming to my house for dinner and a party. Hot dogs and burgers on the grill. Mom didn't make it too busy, had to go see the boyfriend in jail. We had a very good time. Her brothers each gave her a small gift that made her cry. She couldn't remember when she ever had a birthday party, Fred said none of them ever did but that was going to change.

Carolyn stayed with me till the week-end. Saturday I took her over to Fred's house. She showed me her room and said Mary and she picked everything out for the room even the paint. Fred and a friend did the painting. As we put her clothes away she started to cry, we hugged and I had a hard time holding back the tears. Told her she had my phone number and could call everyday if she wanted. But she had made so many new friends when she was here on the week-ends that she would soon fit right in. We said good bye after dinner with a promise that I would come by in 2 weeks to take her out to dinner.

She called me every day at night for the first 4 days to tell me what she did all day. Then every other day. By the time I was to go take her out for dinner she called to say she was going to a sleep over if I didn't mind, but she would call me when she had time.

She has been gone now for 3 months I've seen her twice. She had blossomed in to a beautiful young lady, happy and full of life. She can't wait for Mary to have the baby in a few months so she will be an aunt. GOD does answer prayers.

A week before school was to start Jane from the program called; they have a 13 year old that lived with her grandmother. She had a mind of her own, but was a good kid. Grandma was going into the hospital and would be in rehab for a few weeks could I help. Sara lived in the same area and would be going to her own school. So I said sure.

The next day I went to grandma's to pick her up; nice house, gram was nice Sara looked happy. I asked Gram who was going to be with her at the hospital and if she wanted me to call anyone when it was over. There was only her and Sara. She was worried about Sara so much. The poor thing has been in 1 foster home after another since she was 3 years old. Never know a dad, he was killed in a car accident when Sara was 1 and mom left town 10 years ago and never came back. Gram was all she had left. Gram said she hoped to be home in 4 or 5 weeks. She was having her right knee replaced. Rehab was the longest stay. I told her things would be fine.

Just to be on the safe side I applied for a 6 month temporary custody of Sara. We were set to go. I took Sara to the open house at school; we saw a few friends she knew but not well. School would start on Monday. Sara was close to school so she would walk there and back. I would take her and pick her up if the weather was bad. We went to see Gram at the hospital and gave her flowers Sara had picked from my flower bed. Gram was surprised and happy to see her. We said we would be at the home to see her when she went there in a few days. This made her smile.

Sara was a smart young lady she was doing so well in school, then I got a call from her teacher, there was a lady at the school and wanted to take Sara. When I got to the school the police were there school called them. This was Sara's mother. She wanted her daughter and now. I gave the officer my papers from the courts and told them were Gram was. This woman was mad she didn't even know what Sara looked like she keeps asking ever girl in the hall if she was Sara. The police had to take her to the station. I was to meet them there with Sara.

I called Jane; she met us at the station. Jane went in to talk to Louise about Sara. Louise was living in another state with her on again off again boyfriends. Didn't have a job but had a place at the women's shelter if they needed a place to stay. The police called that police department and was told mom was a hooker; they have been trying to keep her off the streets. She had a court date coming up in a week and wanted the kid so she would stay out of jail. Jane told Louise that we would have to see the judge and he would decide what would happen but until then she would have to go back home and stay away from Sara or go to jail. Our court date was set in 3 weeks. Judge wanted to see what was going to happen to Louise back home first. Police put her on a bus back to Ohio.

Sara knew what was happening and didn't want to see Louise. The officer told her that was fine when he asked her. We went to see Gram she was pretty upset. Told her all would be fine and that Sara wasn't going anywhere. She said the doctor was looking at her charts and hoped she would be able to go home next week. She wanted to be there for Sara. You could tell they really love each other. Sara would sit on the bed telling her all about school and her friends. I left them alone and went to find the doctor. Told her knee was going along fine but they found a lump on her neck and it was stage 2 cancer. They were going to start chemo that day to see if they could control it if not surgery in 3 weeks. Gram would have to have someone come and stay with them when she went home.

We went back to Gram's room to tell them. I knew they were both scared. Gram didn't have a lot of money. She said she would have to see what the insurance company would say to live in help. So she started chemo that afternoon. Sara went with the doctor to do rounds. I told Gram all about Louise and asked if she would like to have her come and help out. No way. Louise was Sara's mother but her dad was Grams son. She never like Louise, she was always bad news. Louise was driving when her son was killed. Told her I was sorry and took Sara home.

I talked to Jane, asked if I would be able to go stay at Grams house and help out till she was better. She only lived 3 blocks from me and I would have free time when the ladies from the church came to sit with her. She said the choice was mine friends help friends all the time. But Sara would still be in my custody for 5 more months.

Sara and I took Gram home that next week. Nurse would come in every day for her shots and take her to chemo. Police came by wile Sara was in school to tell us we didn't have to go to court. Judge in Ohio sent Louise to jail for 18 months. Gram would be fine by then and was planning to move to a smaller house. She put her house up for sale and we started looking for a new one right there and then.

Gram went in for surgery a week later. She is going to be fine. We have started the packing and have shown the house a few times and we have an offer pending. They will come and stay with me till we find just the right house for them. Moving is done we are cleaning for the new owners. They will move in this Saturday. Gram and Sara are so happy things are going their way. Jane came and talk to us about what was Sara's further. What was to happen to her if something happened to Gram. Sara would be 14 in a month but still too young to be alone. Gram and I talked it over. I was put down as next of kin in Gram's will. So I would be looking out for Sara, but Gram is still young only 56 she will be around a long time. Sara was happy with the news when I talked to her, she wanted to know if Gram was ok I told her yes. This was just to be sure she was ok if something did happen. But Gram was still young and would be with us for a long time.

That was 3 years ago and we are going out for Sara's 17th birthday. She is in her last year of high school and hopes to go to the community college next year. Yes we are all still living together at my house so now we are a family.

Carol

The people you meet at a yard sale. I can't understand why some can be so rude. A dear friend passed away and her daughter was trying to get rid of a lot of things before she put the house on the market. Carol is the type of person that if you need something she would give it to you. Libby her mother was just like that and people would walk all over her.

Libby's husband Hank was a lawyer and when he passed away his business went to his two sons from his first marriage, Hank Jr. and Paul. The house and insurance went to Libby and their nine year old daughter Carol. Hank and Libby were married for 16 years and everyone was happy with the will Hank left. Until Carol was out of collage she and Libby would receive a check each month from the business. If Carol went to collage to be a lawyer then she would be given a chair on the board at the office. Carol chooses not to go into law that made the boys happy. Now she was 20 so was on her own.

With a five bedroom house there was a lot of things to sell. First of all Libby was a clothes hog. If she found something she liked she would get one in every color. Hang it up and forget about it. All five bedroom walk-in closet was fill and most of the things still have tags on them. It took days to go through all of them. A lot we gave to the women's shelter that Libby supported. The rest we put out for the sale.

She had a lot of house whole items, costume jewelry most still on their cards or in boxes. Yes we did have them checked out before we put them out. You know when a new 3 piece suit with a tag that says $69.99 on it isn't going to sale for that so we put $5.00 on the tag and hung it on the $5.00 rack, and then someone will say will you take a dollar for it you just say no. There was some bed sets. These was a 4 or 5 pieces sets priced at 500.00 and they would yell at you when you said no to a dollar or two. Yes they were still in store wrap.

There was a group that came together and wile one of them keep us busy the other four stole a lot of clothes and put them in the van were we couldn't see them. The one we were helping then got mad because we wouldn't let her have $75.00 worth of stuff for $10.00 dollars her dropped all the stuff on the ground and left. That is when a friend next door called us and told us what had happened and that she and her husband were following them. They went out to the Flea Market and dropped them off at a booth. Sue said they were laughing and joking about what they stole and were putting tags on them for $20.00 and $30.00 until the police showed up. Sue's husband Jack is a county police officer and had pictures they took of them putting things in the car. Well they will be gone for a while thanks to Sue and Jack.

That was Friday and we made $693.25, Saturday was even better $1203.85. Monday Carol went to the shelter and gave them a check for $2000.00. They were so happy. There was still so much clothes left over that Sue told us to take them to a consignment shop. That was a great plan. So we did. Now we have a house full of furniture, five bedroom sets, Dining room, three front rooms, a game room and still the house. Now I knew Paul and Libby had very good taste in furniture that was why I didn't let Carol sale it at the yard sale. We called a friend that did Estate Sales to come over. After they went all through the house and garage plus the yard we sat and talked about what we had here and what we should do about it. In four weeks we are having an Estate sale and they do all the work. That was the best part. As they started to get thing ready Carol and I moved back over to my house. She took all the things she wanted from the house and put them in storage until she is out of college. Libby left me as power of attorney for Carol till she is 25 years old, in five years. I always tell her she is like a daughter I never had. I don't have children and when my time comes she will get all my things. Only now that I know what has to be done I'm going to start getting rid of things we don't use or need. Plus I will talk to my attorney and make a new will.

I received a call from Hank Jr. telling me not to worry that he and Paul would handle the paper work and finances for us and not to sign anything until they read it. I didn't want a fight so didn't say anything to them. They would be here the day of the sale with all the papers for us to sign. Carol knew how they did her mom, and all they wanted was to spend her money. Carol was not a push over and would take care of things her way.

Two days before the sale Carol and I walked through the house; this was the hardest part for Carol. She had lived here all her life and loved it but it was too big for her. We talked about old times and things that happened there, the parties and the sleep overs out in the yard with her friends. All the good times, we will always have the pictures and memories to keep with us. Soon this will pass and in a few weeks she will be going back to school.

The big day is here. It was a wonderful day about 75 degrees, light wind and no clouds to be seen. Everything was set up.

Carol and I were to sit on the porch to watch what was going on. People started to arrive around 8:00. Their cars were parked for them and 100 chairs were set up. At ten minutes to ten Carol and I took our seats. We saw a lot of old friends and of course Hank and Paul. Right at 10:00 Jeff started things going. He talked about the rules and payment, why we are selling and hoped everyone had a great day. We never been to a sale like this before and just watching was so much fun. Jeff started with the boxes they put together and worked his way up to the furniture. There were times we were laughing and some crying. Sometime we were so surprised at what things sold for, but Jeff knew something about every piece that was there. When and where it was made by whom what it cost at the time and how much it better it was now with age. God bless Jeff, he had things moving right along. By 2:00 most of the things were gone, paid for and moved. All that was left was the house and that would go up for sale at 3:00.

We had about 45 minutes so had time for a little lunch and potty break. Hank and Paul came over to talk, they had all the papers and wanted us to sign them so they could take over. Carol told them she was eating and would talk to them after the house was sold. That didn't make them happy. That was when Hank told Carol not to sale the house that he wanted to move in to it that it was the family home and as much his and Paul's. Jeff spoke up and said that it was set for sale in 10 minutes and if he wanted it to get a number and bid. Mad they walked away and said we would talk when this was over.

Right at 3:00 Jeff started with all the rules. I wasn't surprised to see Hank with a number, Carol said a pray that he didn't get it. They started at $250,000.00 and it keep going up at $495,000.00 Hank stopped bidding. By the time it was over the price went up to 735,000.00. I was speechless and so was Carol. The boys came running over yelling not to sign anything till they read it. They would handle everything. Telling Jeff they wanted all the sheets and papers from the whole sale. Carol told them very loudly NO. That is when they met Mr. Lewis Cook one of the top lawyers in the state. Carol said this is my lawyer and he will take care of things, and since the sale was over they could leave. With that she went into the house and closed the door in their faces. Mr. Cook then informed them that he has been Libby's and Carol's lawyer for a long time and has the papers and Libby's will if they wanted to start any trouble. If they needed anything to see him and to leave Carol alone. I just sat there and smiled.

It took about a week for all the paper work to be done; we took the time to talk about what she wanted to do. She was going to go back to school and get her Masters, then move to England for more school. Carol always loved going with me to England and stay with me at my small cottage on her summer breaks and if she wanted she could live there till she finished with school and wanted to get on with her life. I will miss her very much but she will be home for the holidays as least for the next five years.

I know in my heart that Hank and Libby are pleased with Carol she is a lot like her dad. But has her mother's heart of gold. I sure that Hank is proud with his sons too, they are all good kids I just hope in time they become close and a family. Only time will tell.

Fred

I live on a quiet street in a very nice area, most of the homes were three or four bedrooms with pools and pool house. Before my husband Paul passed he had a great job and we always had guests. Now I'm all alone, but I love my house, my flowers gardens and friends. The only problem is Fred.

Fred is a homeless man that will try and help you. The day of the funeral for Paul we had the luncheon in my yard. When it was over everyone left and I was going to clean the yard tomorrow when they picked up the tables and chairs. I was sitting on the swing when Fred came into the yard. He asked if I had bags for the mess and if I would give him something to eat he would clean the yard for me, didn't want money just food. He looked dirty, smelly, long hair and a beard but I could see his eyes were clean and sharp so I told him the bags were in the garage and to put them in the alley for pick up. If he wanted any of the food left over I would give him some containers to put it in. I put them on the swing and went into the house.

I watch Fred from the dining room table, he was a hard worker and in three hours was done. Put all the tables and chairs on the patio and garbage out. He pack his bag with the food he wanted and by the time I made it out side he was gone. The yard looked wonderful. A week later he was back asking if I needed anything done, I let him work in the flower gardens and I would pay him for it. No he said I only work for food, God takes care of him. So that's how Fred worked for me once a week.

I would have coffee and rolls in the morning and sandwiches for lunch. He would eat at the table and I would use the swing. It was coming on to fall and I asked Fred what he would be doing, we don't get snow in upper Florida but it gets cold for a while. He said he would be heading south for a few months and see if he could find jobs to keep him going. I asked why he didn't go to Hill Top Mission. They would help him with showers, clothes and a place to sleep. He was sleeping under the bridge by the brook and didn't know about the mission. I gave him two sandwiches two apples, and the address and how to get there be for he left for the day.

All that week I was going through Paul's things, I was giving them to church for their yard sale in a few weeks. I set the boxes on the back porch for them to pick up that week-end. The next morning I saw someone in my yard by the flowers, I stepped out on the porch and he turned to look at me. It was Fred, he smiled and said he found the mission and feels like a new man. I made coffee and breakfast told him sorry no rolls today. He looked so nice and I told him so, clean, hair cut short and nice clothes. I'm so happy for him and it made him feel better too. We sat at the table together for lunch, and he started to tell me his story.

He was from Iowa and had two sisters and one brother. Their parents were killed in a fire when he was eight, all the other were younger then him. The twins Carrie and Larry were sent to live with Uncle Roy and Aunt Mary, Betty was sent to Aunt Joan. I was sent to a foster home. I did get to see the others once a month and then one day Uncle Roy told me and Betty that the twins were going to live with new parents and this was the last time we would every see them. It was their third birthday and wouldn't understand, Uncle Roy said they were nice people and would be good parents to them. When Aunt Joan was taking me back to my foster home she said that a nice couple were looking to take Betty in a few weeks but she will get to see me on her birthday before she left. I was hoping that Uncle Roy or Aunt Joan would let me stay with them but Uncle Roy lost his job and they were moving in with Aunt Joan. Since Aunt Mary was going to have a baby she was helping them.

Well Carrie, Larry and Betty all had new moms and dads, and on my birthday I was all along with just my foster parents, they were nice I was giving a card and mom made a cake for me. It was ok I was nine and didn't need much. One day I came home from school and found my stuff packed and my case worker was there, she said I was a good boy but was being sent to a new home. I said my good-byes and we left. My new family had two boys around my age and it made it better to have someone to talk with. I stayed there for a year and on my tenth birthday I was sent to a youth home for boys ten – seventeen. I never stayed in one home for more than a year so I was ready for this move. I would miss the boys and the dog but I was a big boy and people want younger kids.

The home was clean, good food and nice folks, the school was right there so no snow day lost. We all had jobs we had to do. Mine was working in the yard with Jim, he was the one that took care of the gardens, all the food that we could grow we did. We were planting and harvesting something all the time. What we didn't eat we sold on the week-end at a stand in town. I made some nice friends there we had a dorm upstairs and the parents and help slept downstairs. Only ten boys at a time was there. So it was like a great big family. Once a month we would take the family bus into town, each boy was given $10.

oo to spent on what we wanted. You could spend it all or just what you wanted. When we got back home we had to show everyone what we had. Then Jim would open his black book and each of us would give him what money we had left if any. He showed me what they did with it .Every month the state gave us spending money. We could use all of it or try and save some. Two boys Jerry and Glen were going to be fifteen when school was out for the summer, they would start working for some farmers for the next two years and would be making money to save. When they turned seventeen the state would set them up into an apartment and paid two months' rent and helped with a job. After two months they were on their own. When they started their jobs Jim would take them to the bank and open an account in their name. Each week they would go to the bank and put their money into the account, they were allowed to keep $10.00 if they wanted or put it in the bank. The money we would give Jim each month was used to start our accounts on our fifteenth birthday.

That summer when Jerry and Glen started their jobs we all had to move up the job list at home. I was almost twelve so I was moved to the kitchen, there I learned to cook, clean do laundry. I loved when we baked. Then when the gardens were ready we would do a lot of canning for the fall, Mom and Gram were the ones that showed me that task. It was a lot of hard work but they were good to us. They were helping us learn to take care of our self's and it sure helped. In the evenings Jim would take the boys that wanted to help out to his work shop. Jim was a carpenter and would show us how to make things, we would make birdhouses, rockers and footstools. Around Christmas time we would take the stuff to the market to sell as gifts. We were given $1.00 for each item we made and sold. That was our Christmas spending money, we could get something for everyone at the home that was the only time we didn't have to show what we bought. On Christmas Eve we would all bring our gifts down to the tree and in the morning after breakfast Jim would pass them out. We all had a great time.

By the time I was fifteen Jerry and Glen were gone and it was Bobby and mine turn to start working out of the house. Jim took us to the bank and I started with $421.14. That was a lot of money for a fifteen year old. Bobby got a job at the grocery store and I went to Mr. Bean's farm. I worked all summer and in the fall after school for four hours. He was a good boss, showed me a lot about farming and he let me help make the china hutch for his wife's Christmas present. He would always pay for the job you were doing, I made $50.00 a week and I saved most of it. Sometimes I would only keep out $5.00 I didn't need more than that. The home taught us how to do a job right and it paid off. No boy was ever let go from his job for being lazy.

Once we had our jobs done for the day Jim would let those that wanted work in his shop. He really love making things and I did too. He would repair stuff for people or make a new table or chairs. Two months before Christmas we worked on desks, and writing tables for the ladies and rocking horses and dollhouses for the kids. With four of us helping we got a lot done. Jim always paid us something for our help. I loved to smell of fresh cut wood.

By the time lunch was over we didn't get much done, and he had to be back at Hill Top by four or lose his spot in line. So he picked up his two plastic bags and left. Once a week we worked on the yard or cleaning out the pool house. I had the pool put down for the season so I needed the pool house closed up. One day when Fred arrived he looked so down and out, and smelled of smoke. He told me there was a fire at the mission and so far four people were dead and nine in the hospital. No one will be able to stay at the mission it was almost gone. I took him into the house and we made coffee and watched the morning news. They had live on scene coverage and we watch most of the morning. As the death toll keep climbing I could see Fred crying. He knew most that died, by the end of the day nineteen dead and thirty six in the hospital. Plus they found the man that started the fire. He told the police he was mad because he lost his place after two years and set the fire to get even. He was in jail right now but the police think that he will go to the state mental hospital. The police said that the mission and police department would be helping anyone with a place to stay for a few days. Just come to the mission and get help. After we had lunch Fred left with a promise he would let us know what he was going to do. He had about seven folks he would help once a week.

Well I went out to the pool house and started cleaning. I really haven't use it much in the last year or two, but wanted to keep it in shape. The boxes of Paul's clothes were still there I don't know how they were put in the house. I called Hilda from the mission and asked if Fred was there yet, yes he just arrived. Please tell him to come back tomorrow that I found something's for him. I sat out all the clothes so Fred could take what he wanted. Even two suitcases that would be better than the plastic bags. Fred was there at 7a.m. He was to work at the Wilson that day but stopped by here first. I took him to the pool house and told him to take what he wanted. Now Paul wear more sizes then most women do, so there was all sizes there. Fred took what he would need and I told him to put them on the table and he could pick them up when he found a place to stay. He left for the Wilson's and I picked out more things for him, then I called the police department and told them I had a lot of clothes, if they would send someone to pick them up they could have them. They sent a car and he called for a backup, by noon everything was gone. I knew it was going to good use. I went back to my cleaning when I had an idea. Why can't Fred stay here, it had three rooms a very large shower, six people at a time could use it. A small kitchen stove and refrigerator, table and chairs. The other was used for T.V. sofa and a pull out bed. I had other things in my basement that he could use if he wanted. I had it all clean and all I had to do was wait for him to come back.

It was Tuesday when he came back, he said he would be leaving town on Saturday the county was helping move him to another state to a mission. I told him to sit at the table and we would have coffee and rolls. As we ate I told him about my idea that he would be able to stay and help all the people just like he did before the fire. After eating we went out to the house, I put up some curtains and a blanket on the couch. Told him I had pillows and sheets waiting for him to say yes. He said he didn't have much to pay rent and I said just keep helping us older folks and that will do. I told him I had a pot roast cooking and he could stay here tonight and let me know in the morning. So that night he stayed in the now called guest house.

I didn't see Fred till noon, he had to help someone in the morning and was done now. He wanted to talk. He said he was honored that I would do this for him and would be glad to take me up on the offer. That he would give me what money he made for food so he would be helping me too. I was so happy Paul and I never had children and by now Fred was like a son to me. I took him to the basement and told him he could take what he wanted to set up house the way he wanted it. I gave him sheets, towels, dishes and pots and pans. There was a bed down there and he asked if he could use it that he would ask Mr. Dean and his son to help him move it. Dean and Scott came over and helped take the things to the guest house. The next day while Fred was off working Dean came over. He told me that if I didn't mind he and Scott could take out half the shower no one needs one that big and make a small bedroom. I said I would ask Fred and let him know. That night we talked it over and Fred said he would be glad to help them do the work. He even told Dean that he would help do the China Hutch he wanted to make. So for the next two week-ends they were busy, I wasn't to go out there till they were done.

Then one morning Fred ask me to come down for dinner, it would be ready at five. It was his way to show me the work they all did. It looked wonderful he even had a small closet in the bedroom. We had port chops, green beans and salad for dinner. Fred was a good cook. He said that he was starting to work on the hutch and asked if he could use part of the garage to get started that Mr. Dean would bring him the wood. Yes of course and we will look it over after dinner. So we went to the garage and what a surprise for Fred. My Paul had a lot of tools and I told him to use what he wanted. That if there were something's not needed I would pack them up for the church next sale. A few days later he come home from a job and showed me four gallons of white paint, now he could paint the inside of the guest house. I never saw a man that was always working at something. We went to the hardware store and bought a pint of dark green and dark blue paint. I had rollers and brushes in the garage. Fred wasn't one for T.V. so I found a radio for him and you could hear him singing as he worked. The Wilson's were having new carpet put in and ask Fred if he would like the old gray carpet for his house. He asked Wilson to call me and see if it was alright. Now he had carpet and paint for his walls and little time to do things for his self, but he was happy. Finale he started painting first he tinted some light green and did the front room and kitchen. The next day he tinted the blue and did the bathroom and a little darker blue for the bedroom. The rest of the week he was off to work somewhere.

That Saturday Scott came over and they laid the carpet in the three rooms. If you were to see this house two months ago you would not believe what it looked like now. Now he added the full size bed and dresser to the room and all was set. Once a week he would knock on the back door and ask what I needed done today. We went to the hardware store and found fall flowers to put out in my gardens. We worked all day at it and went out for dinner. All day he would be gone helping someone and at night in the garage working on something. I had a heater put in because fall was on its way and he was working on the hutch plus other things people needed fixed or made. Fred stayed there for two years and one night at dinner I asked how he became homeless, so he told the rest of the story.

At seventeen he was given an apartment and a job. He worked in a steel molding factory. They made molds for drills and saws. He tried to make friends but didn't like all the swearing and smoking they did or to go sit at the bars half the night. So he would just work and go home. After four months the boss came to me and said he had to let me go, that the guys didn't like me being around and he didn't want to loss most of them. He gave me two weeks' pay and a letter of recommendation for work. Jobs were hard to find and before too long I was out of money then the apartment went and next the car. So at seventeen I was out on the streets and been there since. I never did ask him before how old he was till now. He looked at me and said twenty six. Been on his own till now. I told him he would always have a home here.

One afternoon a gentleman came looking for Fred, he was in his work shop so I sent him out there. I called Fred on the intercom to let him know someone was looking for him. I didn't see the man leave but when Fred came in for lunch he looked happy and sad. I knew he would tell me what happened when he was ready. Finale he said that the man was a friend of Mr. Dean's and saw the hutch he made for them, He told Fred he had a small company in the Panhandle and sure could use more help if he was interested. He only had four others working for him and all good people. Would Fred like to come and take a look? He left his card and asked him to think it over and give him a call by Friday. He asked what he should do. I told him he had to start thinking of himself, and only the good Lord knew how long I would be around. If he wanted to go and look around I would be glad to take him. Dean came over to talk to him to tell him to think about it that Mr. Larson was a good man and keeps his promises. Two days later he called Mr. Larson and said we would like to come down next Friday if he had time for us. Sure come on over.

Mr. Larson met us in his office and would give us a tour of the factory. We put on eye glasses and hard hats then went out into the shop. So many machines and all kinds of wood. It smelled like a forest. We met one man at a time and he showed us what he was doing and what it would be. We watched each of them and how they did it. As we went to the last man he was making a design on a table top it was beautiful, as he turned to look at us a big smile crossed his face. He turn off his saw and gave Fred a big hug. They were both laughing and crying that made all the men stopped working and came over. It was Jerry one of the boys that Fred met at the youth home. Mr. Larson took all of us into the break room and ordered lunch. Jerry told everyone that this was the boy he was always talking about. He felt like they were brothers and so sorry he lost touch with him when he turned seventeen. Lunch came and we had a nice visit then the men went back to work.

Mr. Larson told us he found Jerry ten years ago and he was still here, plus Jerry married his daughter and gave him three grandkids. He was one very happy man. He said Jim did a great job showing them how to do a job and do it right. Then he asked Fred if he would like to move there and work with the guys? Fred asked if he could think about it over the week-end and looked at me I only smiled. Mr. Larson said yes and Fred asked if he would have Jerry call him this Saturday. Then we started home. Fred was quite for a long time then asked what should I do? He was worried about me and the people he had been helping for so long. Told him it was up to him that he needed to get on with his life, plus he had a friend there and they liked the same work. We would go back to doing things ourselves like before we met him. Jerry called and they talked for hours, Jerry had a guest apartment over his garage and Fred could live there as long as he wanted.

All week we didn't talk about it then Friday morning he came in for coffee and rolls, he said he was calling Mr. Larson and taking the job I was so happy for him. He told Mr. Larson he had a few jobs that he needed to do first then would be ready to move in a week to ten days. Jerry called that night and said his wife was so happy he was coming and couldn't wait to meet him. It felt so right, yet I knew in my heart I would miss him badly. Jerry and his family came to dinner on Sunday. I made a pot roast and we had a nice visit. Jerry and Fred went out to the garage and Karen and I did the dishes while the three kids played. I asked what was in the apartment and what Fred would need. Only thing was a stove and refrigerator, I said fine he could take everything in the guest house with him. We went to look at the things Fred had. While we were looking around we went into the garage and told them if there were any tools he wanted to please take them because I was having the church come over and take what they wanted. Told Jerry if he wanted some to just tell Fred. Karen told Jerry he would have to bring one of dad's big truck to pick up Fred because he had all the stuff in the house to pack too.

In the week that followed we did a lot of packing and added things from the basement for him to take with. He would ask if the tools he was taking were ok then pack the box. All the packing was done by Friday and that night all Fred's friends came over for a pot luck cook out just to say thank you to Fred. I didn't know he helped so many people. On Saturday Jerry came with a very big truck, Scott and Dean came over to help with the loading. In three hours they were done. Fred asked me to come to the guest house to check things out. When I got there he uncovered a beautiful rocking chair he made it for me so I would always remember him. It was to thank me for being a mom he never had and he would keep in touch. Jerry took the chair into the house for me, we had a quick lunch, said our good-byes and they left. That was four years ago.

Every Mother's Day I would receive flowers to the best mom in the world. Once in a while He would come for the week-end or I would go there. One week-end he came with a very pretty young lady, her name was June he said they were going to be married and would I come to the wedding. I was so happy for them, they looked so in love. I was to start at Mr. and Mrs. Larson's for the week-end and the wedding was to be in the yard. It was a great day for a wedding. Everyone was happy for them. They would stay in the apartment until they could buy a house. Both had good jobs and knew how to save so I knew it wouldn't be for long.

We still write and visit, last week they gave me a table to match my rocker. Yes I will never forget Fred, he was a gift from God for so many people.

Lee's One Stop

The alarm went off at 4:15 time to get up. Wish I could turn over and sleep one more hour. But we have a store to open the first of June and I still have to get it ready. So up shower and dressed.

Here it was March already and we still had so much to do. I picked up Clara and we started to Lee. It was a small town about 6 miles from where we lived. The snow was melting and all we had was mud were we parked. The city said they were putting gravel down Saturday and here it was Monday. Clara started the coffee and I turned on the heat.

We had our coffee and donuts and were ready to start when 2 city trucks pulled up with the gravel. They had to pull my car out of the mud first. Pete wasn't too happy we were there already. I told him I wasn't happy he didn't do it Saturday. After five minutes of yelling I went back inside.

We set up the ladders and started scraping the old paint off the walls. By lunch time the place was warm. The man from the freezer company was to be here at 2:00 to finalize were the walk in cooler freezer was going and were the compressors would be. As we ate we talked about the store. 2 more months and we open, My God so much to do. Mr. Carter arrived I signed the papers and all will be here Wednesday. I call Mr. Turner to let him know about what time so he could be here with the crane. All was going fine.

Friday my partner and I went to the bank, more papers. Mr. Swanson was my silent partner so we went to a bank out of town. From the bank to lunch, we had just put more money in my store account.

Ground breaking was Tuesday for the gas tanks. Tanks will be here Thursday and the crew to put them in on Friday. The inspector will be here both days to watch what they do, so I don't have to worry.

Clara and her girls made sandwiches and soup at home and were here in time for lunch. Freezer was working, Tanks are almost done and painting starts Saturday. Should have that all done by March 30th.

After the painting was done things started going so fast. The shelves were set up, they were building the counters and office was put in. Phones were working; supplies started arriving we worked from 7am till 6pm. Next week the ovens and appliances will be here and set up. We had to start using the back door because the drive and pumps were being put in.

April came and went so fast I didn't know where it had gone. Everything was great our sign was put up today. The Mayor and City Council will be here tonight to check us out. The City inspector and gas company has okayed everything.

Clara and I sat out snacks and coffee for everyone. The Mayor was pleased with how things looked. He handed me our permits and the fire chef gave us 2 fire exit signs. Said to be sure they go up tomorrow.

May 20th. Gas truck will be here today, food and venders will start tomorrow. Cases are all cleaned, Ovens are ready and the donut machine is ready to go. May 31st we are having an open house. June 2nt will be out first day of business.

Saturday the 31st Clara and her girls got here just before 7am. We will open the doors at 11am for the open house. Clara is in the kitchen making donuts, Kathy is cutting meat for sandwiches wile Barb and I make tea, coffee, and punch. Tables are set and ready to go.

Mayor and most of the town was there for the ribbon cutting. Reporters from the 2 towns around us were here too. Everyone smiled as we cut the ribbon and opened the doors. Wayne's Greenhouse came by with flowers and plants as a house warming gift for the store. He even planted them for us nice of him. Starting June 2nd we will be open 6am to 7pm 6 days a week. Closed Sunday. We have to wait 6 months before we can get our wine and beer license.

The first few weeks we were very busy. Everyone came to see the new store and ask questions. School was out for summer and the store was right across the street from the park. Parents and kids were in and out for donuts or drinks. All summer went well. We'll miss all of them next week when school starts.

Today is October 5th we have been open 4 months, it has not been easy. We are making it month by month still in the black. I was in the office when Clara came in she wanted to know what was wrong. I told her the truth that we are above water at the time but winter will be here soon and if it snows hard I don't know if we will make it to work. Plus I was having troubles at home. Paul my husband was not happy I was here so much and not home. I told him I can't hire anyone yet we were just making it with her and me. Clara said Kathy and Barb would be happy to come over 4 or 5 hours in the evening and close up for us. I could pay them what we could. I said I would think about it.

I picked up two fold up beds, blankets, pillows and quilts. Just in case. Things were starting to look up. The girls worked 4 days a week from 3-7. That gave Clara and me a little time for us. We even had orders coming in for Halloween parties plus the Lee Fall Fair would be here from the 2nd-10th in November. People come from all over to the fair.

From October 20th till November 12 we were busy, I had to call for more gas drops every week. With the sandwich trays and donut orders coming in and they wanted for us to make cookies too. I had to have to girls work every day with us. We had people from all over. I even put up a bucket for names and phone numbers, each month I would have a customer pull a name and that person would get a free doz. donuts. Then I would pitch that months names and start over again.

By the time the 12th of November was there we had 12 orders for Turkey Dinners. Each dinner would have 1 turkey or ham, mashed potatoes, dressing, grave, cranberries, candy carrots and dinner rolls. Everything had to be picked up by 6:00 Wednesday night. We would be closed Thursday. Orders keep coming in.

I ordered containers for everything. Went out to the turkey farm and ordered the birds, 26 turkeys. Then the grocery store, 12 hams, 2 50lb's bags potatoes, a case of fresh cranberries and 2 cases of carrots and everything we needed for the dressing. Starting Monday we will start cooking.

November 19th Monday after Clara finished the donuts and the kitchen was clean we started with the dinners. Kathy started with the carrots, first cleaned them and cut in slices. Barb started with the potatoes. Had to be sure they were all cleaned. Tomorrow we will cook the cranberries and package them in the containers and put in the cooler till ready to pack the orders. We'll cook the carrots cut celery, onions and be ready for Wednesday to make the dressing.

Tuesday we cleaned the turkeys, put them in foil pans and in cooler. Kathy took the necks and gizzards to boil for the grave and dressing. Carrots and cranberries cooked, packed in cooler.

Wednesday morning started cooking turkeys boy did the store smell so good. Bread vender arrived with 75 packages of dinner rolls. I hope that is enough. By 10'clock food was cooking everywhere. Potatoes were ready and packed; the first 8 turkeys were done and ready to go. Put 10 more turkeys and 5 hams in now. First orders will be picked up at 4. We are rolling along fine. By 2:30 last of turkeys and hams in ovens. Took some ham out of sandwich case and made us dinner. Cleaned up kitchen and made ready to close. We were all so tired, so glad when 7pm arrived we were ready to go home.

Thanksgiving Day Clara and the girls came to my house for dinner; I made a turkey and pot roast just in case we were tired of turkey. It was so nice and warm that we had doors and windows open. Paul and Barb's boyfriend Clay was watch football we were in the kitchen working on Christmas dinners and New Year's. We needed a head start Christmas was only 4 weeks away.

Saturday I was in the office paying bills and doing payroll when Kathy came in. As we were getting the bank deposit ready I told her this was the first month we made a profit. I hope December would do as well or better. Kathy left for the bank; Clara and Barb were cleaning when Mr. and Mrs. Taylor came in and wanted to talk to me. They had one of our ham dinners and I was hoping it was good. Yes all was fine with the dinner, but could I possible consider making the food for their daughter's wedding in February. They were renting the Fellowship Hall and needed someone to do the food. The people that were going to backed out and had moved. All we had to do was the cooking there were others to set up, do the serving then clean up. I just had to cook the food. I told them I would let them know on Monday. Kathy came back and the four of us talked it over and Kathy would talk with them on Monday see what they wanted and figure out the cost. Then we would let them know. Rest of the day was fine.

2 weeks before Christmas it started to snow. We were busy and had orders everywhere. All kind of parties, Orders for Christmas dinners and New Year's orders coming in. I had to bring in seasonal workers. That sure was a big help. I was hoping to train them for the kitchen, and counter. I told Clara if they worked out we would have someone here in town if the roads got bad. We were lucky the snow was light and weather looked good till January.

2 days before Christmas we started the dinners. We took on too much, 31 turkeys, 17 Hams and 15 sandwich trays. But with a few more girls from the high school we made it. Closed

Christmas Eve at 4pm. We are going to Clara's for Christmas. Gave Betty and Grace their gifts and the two school girls too. Asked who was going to be here to help for New Years. School girls said no but Betty and Grace said yes. After the first of the year I will talk to them about working part time.

New Year's was a lot better, only 16 turkeys, 7 Hams and 21 trays. By now we are pros at this. Closed up at 4 on New Year's Eve and headed home. Paul wasn't feeling well so we stayed home. I was beat so it was fine with me. Next day I sat in my kitchen doing the books. Writing out end of the year bills and couldn't believe what we had made. If things keep up we will be fine all winter. Paul still wasn't feeling well so we had a light dinner and off to bed.

Clara and I were at the store by 5:30, girls would be here later. Venders from the beer and wine companies will be here to start taking orders. Called the Mayor asking if he wanted this to start? I didn't care if we did or not. We had a good business going and got by without it so far. He wanted the beer and wine so we will. Paul called from work and said he was going to see the doctor when he got into town. I told him I would go with but he said no he would call me after. Doctor told him that he ate too much holiday eating and a lot of folks were sick and the flu was going around.

Talked to Betty and Grace, they will be staying on I will show them how to open and run the store If we can't make it. So far weather is still good. A little snow now and then but not much stays. The ladies are doing a great job; Clara and I are going to start taking Wednesdays off Betty and Kathy work mornings 5:30 till 2 and Grace and Barb from 2 till 7. Can't believe in only 6 months we went from 2 people to 6 working here. By the 15th the wine and beer was set. Had our liquor license and ready to go. Mayor was first to buy the beer. All was great.

Sunday night Paul had a headache and went to bed early. I followed soon after. Paul leaves for work at 2am so he is home by 11:30am. As I was getting up to get ready for work I felt someone in my bed. I jumped up and turned on the light it was Paul. This is at 4:30. He said he was sick so came back home. He didn't look good so I called Clara. She would take Kathy in with her this morning. I was going to take Paul to see the doctor.

Called the doctor's office at 8am told Linda that Paul's arms and back hurt, I was told to bring him right in. Doc. Did an EKG and said he was having a heart attack and he called the ambulance. The EMT'S took him to Beckford Hospital. They ran tests and next day he was sent to surgery. He had open heart, 4 arteries were blocked. The specialist said Paul had been have small strokes for a while. All we can do is pray he will be fine. I stayed at the hospital night and day for a week. Clara would bring me clothes and tell me how things were at the store. Kathy did the books and Clara would bring me the checks to sign. Paul was very weak. Doc. Said he would be there for at least 3 weeks. I told Paul I was going home and would be back in the evenings to see him.

Paul was getting better; we were planning to bring him home a week early. Clara and the girls helped me clean the house, put clean sheets on the bed for him and put the TV in the bedroom. He was spoiled at the hospital. I was happy to leave for Beckford at 10:30 to get him. As I was heading for his room the nurse told me the doctor was waiting for me in the office. There is always paper work and orders to take with you. Not today, Paul was in the bathroom getting dressed and had a heart attack. He was dead by the time they found him. I was stunned I didn't know what to do; I called Clara she was there in an hour for me.

Thank God I had Kathy, Barb, Betty and Grace. Kathy and Barb took over the store. I had so much to do families to call and Paul's work. Clara went with me to the funeral home. All the plans were set. People were coming in day and night. The day of the funeral we closed the store. Our church put on the luncheon after the service at the cemetery. The Pastor told me he was there if I needed him, all I could keep thinking is if I was home with him more he may still be here. I knew it would take time but I would get better.

For the next week there was so much to do. I found out many things about Paul that I didn't believe. Plus I had to do the house bills and found out half were behind. Thank God for his insurance money. It saved me from filing bankruptcy. I made it; soon I was ready to go back to work.

Everyone was so kind. But I was so glad to be back. I had forgotten about the wedding in February. Kathy, Barb and Clara didn't. They had the food ordered and everything ready to go. I didn't have a thing to do. I did help in the kitchen cooking the day before but they did the rest.

February 15th. It started to snow 2 week after we put Paul to rest. It looked so cold out there and I knew Paul didn't like cold. But I knew he was nice and warm upstairs with GOD. It snowed off and on for 3 days. Sometimes light, then heavy. Before long we had 2 feet of snow, so far the roads were fine. Had to wait for the gas tanker driver he was running late because of the weather. I needed the gas so we played cards waiting for him.

11:30 we heard the truck. Gene filled the tanks and we packed him some coffee and sandwiches to go. By now the roads were blown over and we had country roads to drive not safe. First time we will be staying at the store for the night.

By morning there was more snow then I've seen in years. Called Betty and told her to stay home. We opened not sure if anyone would be in but the farmers and their John Deer tractors can go any were. Around noon the city boys came in and said the roads were open if we were going home. But to be careful because more snow was coming. Talked to the ladies and after we closed dropped the keys off at Betty's. Didn't know if we would be in the next day. We were stranded at home for 2 days and it felt good to just rest.

It snowed until March off and on. Farmers were happy for the water. As we sat at work for lunch I said to Clara that we have made a round circle. Here it was March again and we were starting into our second year. We decided that in June we would have a Party thanking everyone for their support. Yes things were looking up. I know things will happen, and there will be times that I will want to pull out my hair. Then I look around and see all we have done.

Again today it started to snow. One more blast the weather man said this going to be heavy at least 1 to 2 feet. Another night sleeping at the store. Used to it now so we went to bed early. About 11pm the phone was ringing and someone was banging on the door. County Police, they had a family that's car was stuck in a ditch and they couldn't get a tow truck out till light. Asked if they could stay with us. Roads were bad and the police were busy. Sure we would keep them warm. We watched some truckers and plows running up and down the street. Fix some food for the Millers, and took the blankets off the beds for them to lie on. Just as we were getting settled in there was a horn blowing and in came Chuck. He saw the lights on and was going to ask Clara and me to come to his farm for the night. Told him about the family asked if he would let them go over, there were 5 kids and they needed a warm place to sleep. He took all 7 to his 4 bedroom farm and said he would pull their car out in the morning. That is what good people do.

Next day sun was out, plows were running we were selling lots of donuts, coffee was free today. Day after tomorrow is April the 1st. summer is right around the corner. Chuck and the Millers came in and the family stayed with me till Chuck and dad got the car out. Mrs. Miller was praying to be able to get to Ohio before dark, they were on their way to her dads, lost their home and jobs so were going to stay with him for a while. Hour later the men were back. Mr. Miller took his wife outside to talk to her. A few minutes later they came back in and told us they were going to stay at Chuck's for a few days till the weather broke. He was going to help around the farm for room and board for the family. After rolls and donuts everyone left.

The weather was hit and misses for a week. Then one morning the sun was bright and it was so nice out that you can hear the birds signing. The roads were clear and all was alright with the world. Next day the Millers were leaving town, thanked everyone for their help. I put a full tank of gas in the car and made sandwiches and hot coco for the kids. Gave them my number and asked them to call when they made it to Ohio. Two days later she called, her dad met them in Gary Indiana were they spent the night then on to his house.

Spring was in the air and all was good. I had made a lot of good friends, a wonderful business; I would be able to start paying my silent partner off sooner than we were thinking. Clara, Kathy, Barb and I were talking about the girls starting a catering business. They would work out of the store. Never know what will happen next. All is right with the world.

My Early Years

The only happy time I had in my young life was when I lived with my grandma. I was born to an unwed mother and not wanted. But gram loved me so I stayed with her till I was 6 then went to stay with mom and my stepfather. I now had 2 sisters and a brother.

Time passes and lives change. Mom divorced Carl and married an older man. We moved to a small town and they had 3 more kids. 2 more girls and a boy. 7 kids in all 11 years between me and baby Glen. I started babysitting when I was 13 so both of them could work, times were hard and Bill's health wasn't good. When I was 16 he had a heart attack and couldn't work. He was in and out of the hospital a lot so I quit school got a job and helped take care of the family. I made a mistake and had a baby when I was 20. But I stayed and took care of the family instead of getting married. Two years later Bill died.

By now mom's health wasn't doing so well Dr. Kool said she couldn't work much so here I was with a family to support. Candy, Patsy and Brother Ben were all married by now so that only left 4 kids and mom to care for. I stayed there for a few years till mom was back on her feet. Where I was working I met a man he was divorced and was looking for someone to help him with his kids over the summer and I was looking for a dad for my son. He had 6 kids but only 3 he would have for the summer. The kids at home were working and mom was back on her feet so we got married in December.

We moved to a small town where he got a job as a police officer. As soon as school was out he went and picked up the kids. Jim and Jane were married and Jr. had a summer job. Laure had summer school so only Jake 15, Dick 14 and Jacky 12 came. With my son 14 that was 4 kids. I should be able to handle this wrong. His kids didn't like my son Ronny or me. When Ray was home they were as sweet as honey but when he left for work all hell broke loose. Swearing toughing things braking things until it was time for dad to come home for lunch. An hour peace.

One day Ray forgot his ticket book at home and came to get it he was standing at the door just in time to see a pillow from the couch hit a picture on the wall and the kids yelling and laughing because it broke. Jake was saying poor Sherry now she has to get a new one when he walked in the door. Everyone was quite he went into the bedroom and called me, how long has this been going on? All I could say was from day one. He said we would talk when he came home for dinner. As he left he told them to clean up the mess and he would see them at dinner. After dinner he made them do the dishes and sweep up the floors. Even Miss Jacky couldn't talk her way out of it.

After they went to their rooms we talked, I told him that they could hear us in the vents so we went out into the back yard to the swing under the tree. We could see the windows from there. He started asking questions and I told him the truth. Why didn't I tell him what was going on, because they were angels when he was home and all lovey dove when he was here so who would he believe. I told him I'm not sure how much more Ronny and I can take. It isn't fair to Ronny to get blamed for everything that happens even if Ronny said it was ok.

The next day he was off so at 9:00 he went upstairs and sent Ronny down. I could hear him in the vent telling them they had 1 week to straighten up or he was taking them. We were to go to the fair that day but because they did wrong we were staying home. He called Joe and talked to him for a few minutes then told Ronny to go change clothes. Half hour later Joe and his family pulled up Ronny, Ray took Ronny out to the car gave Joe money and Ronny went to the fair with them. I knew Joe and Betty and knew he was in good hands. To say the least the others were not happy. Ray made to boys help him with the yard work and Jacky have to help with the beds and laundry not a happy girl.

For two days things were fine then I made spaghetti for dinner, Ray was working the night shift and his dinner hour was at 9:00 so it was something I could heat up for him. Jake decided he didn't want it so he thought his plate at the wall, then the other two did the same. Someone turned over the large bowl and it was all over the table sauce too. I took Ronny by the hand and went to the park. That is where Ray found us while he was on patrol. He took us home and you could see they tried to clean the wall but spaghetti sauce stains.

They were all in the front room and I told Ray I was taking my son and leaving the next day. I didn't care what he did with his kids I couldn't take it anymore. Then I went into my room. I called Betty and asked if Ronny could stay there over night she knew what was going on and I didn't want him there with these kids. I was afraid for him, she came right over and picked him up I packed a bag. Ray had to go back to work. He didn't wake me till morning there was some trouble in town and he had to work over. I made breakfast and we talked. He did a lot of thinking and told me he always knew something was wrong but I never said anything so he let it go. He was sorry and would I stay. I had to think on it. He called the kids mom, she wasn't happy but he told her they would be home by 4:00. He call the kids down to eat and then went upstairs with them to get their things. He had them bring stuff down and put out on the porch, when all was done they loaded the car he said he would be back by 7 to wait dinner for him and bring Ronny home.

I picked up Ronny had to tell Betty what happened all day and then we went to the hardware store for paint for the dining room. Half the town knew what happened. The next day after Ray left for work the doorbell rang, there were 6 young people standing there with rollers and tarps they came to help me paint. They were friends of Ronny's. So from 8:00 till noon we painted the dining room and the hall. I ordered pizza and soda for lunch and we had a great time. Ray get there as the pizza arrived so he ate with us. He let the kids know they did a great job and that Saturday to come by and he would pay them. Carrie said you just did, we gave them lunch and they were friends of Ronny's and friends help friends.

Three weeks later June called Jake took off, he and 3 others stole a car and robbed a gas station. The police were looking for them was he here. Ray said no but if they showed up he would arrest them. Then after she told him it was all my fault he hung up on her. He called the Chief and told him what happened, this time he would go to jail. Every day she would call and tell me what a rotten person I was, then she would call the police dept. and complain about Ray. One night the chief came to talk to us. This didn't look good for the dept. So we decided that it would be best if we left town then she would stop her calling.

So we moved to Alden and he got a job with a vending company. I went to work for a dept. store and things were looking up. The next 3 years were fine Ronny turned 18 and wanted to be on his own so he and a friend got jobs and a small apartment. Ray and I had saved some money and brought a house since we were getting up in years. Ray wanted to retire at 55 and he was 7 years older so why not. The next few years were fine Ray even like his job so he kept working.

Then one day I received a letter and about 25 pictures in it. There were pictures of his vending truck parked next to his ex-wife's house. I read the letter it said that he was there every week for the last 3 or 4 years and he thought it was time I knew if I didn't already. I waited till lunch and sat the pictures and letter by his plate then called him in to eat. I just sat there eating my sandwich not saying a word till he was done reading the letter. All I asked was why, he told me she was lonely and was having problems with Jacky and Dick so he would stop by with the child support and check on things. Okay but why were you there for more than an hour when you were to be working? I told him we didn't pay support since Jacky turned 18, three years ago.

I needed time to think, finally I told him I wanted a divorce, I told him I didn't trust him we would sale of house and he could go back to her if that is what he wanted. I was going to make an appointment next week to see the lawyer. Then I went bowling with my team. He was asleep when I returned home. Saturday and Sunday I was busy with church we were getting ready for our yearly yard sale. Sunday night I ask what things did he want from the house and if he talked to June about going south. He didn't want anything and she didn't want to move so he was going to stay with his sister.

I made the appointment for Thursday. Wednesday morning he came into my bedroom and said he didn't feel well. It wasn't like Ray to miss work so I looked at him and he looked like ash I call Dr. Smith's and he met us at the office, took an EKG and told us there was an ambulance on the way he was having a heart attack. The Doctor at the hospital told us he would have to have a 3 or 4 by-passes. We had to do something now. I called his oldest son Jim and he came to the hospital. Early the next morning he went into surgery. It took 6 hours before the doctor came out. He said Ray's heart was bad and we will have to wait and see if he makes it through the night, I stayed at the hospital till I knew he was out of the woods. By noon the doctor said he was better and I needed to go home they would call if we were needed. By tomorrow we would know more.

I called work and told them I didn't know when or if I would be back. Mr. Timme's said just call on Mondays with an update. Ray's boss said his insurance would cover all of this so not to worry. He was in the hospital for 3 and a half weeks. Doctor said he would be off work for 6 to 8 months and if he still had problems not return at all. He keep having trouble with his lungs and the doctor said if we didn't move to warmer weather he wouldn't make it a year or two. So I called my sister in Greensburg P.A and asked her to start looking for a small house for us. I put our house up for sale in November. We were going to Sally's house for Christmas to look around. If I left him who would watch over him not his 86 year old sister who wasn't doing well herself.

We went down on the 22nd of December staying till January 10th. I was hoping we would find something then. I received four calls from Mary about our house she had showed it 3 times but not sure about the price. The same house across the street sold for $40,000.00 more than I was asking so we waited. In March we had a bid on the house so we went back to Saly's. Found a house at the end of the block nice and quiet. We put in our bid pending the sale of our house. Now we sit and wait. Three days later Ann called and said they would take it. Wrote a holding check and went back home. I was to call when things went through.

Mary keep trying to get me to drop the price and I said no. $149,000 was the price and that was it. I went shopping and she came to the house to show it again to the same people and Ray dropped the price to $125,000 He sold the house. I didn't talk to him for a week. When I saw Mary at church she was sorry she even came over to me, she was so happy she sold the house for us. Tried to hug me and I gave her both barrels' First I told her she had no right to drop the price without both of us agreeing to it my name was on the papers too. Also Dr. Smith and I told her Ray was not in his right mind to do things on his own. Dr. Smith even wrote her a letter on it. I was not happy and now how was I to pay off the house in Greensburg. Was she giving me the money, no you didn't do me any favors only made things worse. So stay away from me. I left her standing there with everyone looking at her. Dr. Smith called me when He got home and asked if I was ok, that was the first time anyone told Mary off and in church.

May 26th we signed the papers selling the house somehow the Realty Estate Board heard what happened and someone else was there for the sale. We also received check from this man for over $7,000. That was Mary's commission, no closing cost and no fees. I took it and ran. We had the car and a large moving truck rented, my brother was coming tomorrow to drive the truck then he would fly back. We stayed with friends and left in the morning. Drove from Illinois to Ohio spent the night had breakfast then by 5 hit the road. Made it to Greensburg by noon.

Sally and her family and friends were at the house waiting for us. As soon as we said hi to everyone all started unloading the truck. Sally and I had this all figured out the bedrooms was the last things to go on the truck and first off. I stood in the hall and as they came in I told them what room to go too. As all the parts were there they put up the beds, boxes were marked guest room and master soon as the boxes were there Sally's mother- in –law Pat opened and made the beds. Front room and kitchen next by 7'o clock on May 28th 1994 we were moved it. Sally had diner in the oven and food in the refrigerator. Plus beer for the guys and soda for us. Everyone left at 9 and we were home and in bed by 10. Bert stayed till June 3rd. then flew home he was a great help our garage was pack with boxes. Up north I had 4 bedrooms, a den, family room and basement. Here we had 3 bedroom, front room and small kitchen and no basement boy did I have a lot to think about. Things work out for the best so we started a new life in the Greensburg.

Ray's health got better, by the next year he wanted to go back to work so we went to see a doctor and had him checked out. Doc. gave him an okay. Just be careful. I had an independent contractor job with the post office, I worked out of the south side office. The job was from 7 am till 2 so I had Ray put on my route as my sub. I worked 3 days he worked 3. That was doing fine. Then one day I was delivering a package to a 2nd flood and as I was coming back down, a mob of little kids came running down and I fall the rest of the way down. The next thing I remember I was in the hospital. The post office called Ray, Sally took him to finish the route and she came to the hospital. I had a broken leg and ankle. I had to be off my feet for a month or more. Since we used our own car he had a way back home. I called the post office and told them that Ray would be taking over the route till I could get back. I still had 3 years on my contract.

Then I called my boss at the main post office told Glen what happened and I had it covered, if Ray couldn't handle it I was going to hire my sister so I sent her in to be printed and picture taken. After her papers came back from the FBI she could start work. All went very well. They took turns, Ray trained her for a week when Ray had to see the doctor or go for tests Sally would work. My friend next door would come over every morning help me dress, make me eat then push me over to her house. Her husband George build two ramps one for my house one for theirs. We would work in her sewing room from 9 till Ray came home. That summer we made 14 quilts even one for me. Soon I was back on my feet and ready to work, Ray wanted to keep the post office and the money I paid Sally was a big help to her so I went to work at the grocery store. I liked Mike's I made a lot of friends there.

Before you knew it I had 6 months left of my contract and we had to put in bids in 3 months. They sent you a spread and you need to fill in all the blanks. That would tell they how much they needed to pay you each month. Then you had 2 months to wait to hear from them to see if your bid made it or not. So June 2004 I was told that the bid went to someone else and I would have to train him in two weeks. That I was doing a great job but his bid was under mine. I told my boss at the store I would have to work night for a week or two till his training was over. That was fine with him. When I was ready to start days again he was going to train me for the office. All was working out fine.

I trained Jim for two weeks then he was on his own. Told him if he needed help to call Ray or Sally they would still have their badges for a year and they could sub for him. I think he called them 3 or 4 times. I started the next week at a store in the next town over. You can't train for an office or manager job were you're going to work. So for two weeks it was fun. Soon I was back at my store and the boss called me into the office. First I want you to forget everything they said. We do things here my way. So you will be working for a week with Nancy, she will show you my way, fine I would be okay, Mike's was buying up stores and I had to going up state for a month to convert 2 of them to Mike's. One store was easy but the other one didn't like someone telling them they had to learn a new way. I would go in at 7 am and have to redo the safe and paper work. After a week I called the District Manager and told him what was going on. I only had a week left and I wanted to go home. I didn't work week-ends so Monday morning he met me at the door with the manager and CSM to open the store. We went right to the office and he started opening drawers and wanted to see the safe. I was to stand back and watch.

Oh my, he was upset. He had been to the first store I did and they were running fine so what happened here? I told him I was fighting a losing battle I would work all day putting it in order and the next day I had to start over. He called receiving and wanted boxes then took everything out of the filing cabinets. Then had the baggers put the boxes in his van. Three filing cabinets were removed from the office, the office work deck was moved so she could see the people and help them when they came to the counter. They didn't have to wait any more. He was having the wall in the manager's office taken half way down and glass put in so they couldn't go in and close the door.

By noon everyone was there, he called roll call. Then he started with the new Mike's rules. Their uniforms would be here Monday on the truck, Name tags were ready and to be worn now. He was having someone from each department from other stores coming to this one to show them what he wanted if they wanted their jobs it was Mike's way or out the door. It was up to them. He would be back in a few weeks to see the change. I stayed two more week because I had to train a new office clerk and CSM. He let the others go. So we had a new Manager, asst. manager and CSM and office clerk on Monday to open the store. I knew Carl the asst. Manger I worked at a store with him. And he knew his job I was pleased, I went home.

I had a week off for R&R I needed it my legs were hurting so bad by bed time it was hard to walk. So I went to see a doctor were Ray went. He was going to run an angiogram to see what was wrong with my legs. If he could he would put in a stent or two to help me. I was back in the holding area with my sister when he came in. There was nothing he could do at this time but I had to see a heart specialist he had someone on the way. Sally got all upset but I told her this was a piece of cake till Dr. Wood walked in. He told us that the widow maker artery was 90 percent blocked and he had me set for surgery on Wednesday at 7 am. Be back here at 6:00 sharp. His nurse would call me at home with orders. I told Sally he was one good looking doctor but made his point very clear. Sally stay till Ray came home told him what was going on and she would be back with dinner and would stay the night if I wanted. I said no but she slept on the couch anyway. So I had a baby sitter for two days.

Wednesday May 10, 2006 She helped with my shower and getting dressed we were at the hospital at 5:45 Ray went to work. He didn't want to be here it reminded him of his. Sally was to call when it was over. Marie from next door and my friend Carol were there too. I was fine. When I was taken into the operation room the nurse asked if I took me meds I said no, well your blood pressure is doing fine and she was surprise. I looked at her a said if you had one hell of a good looking doctor like Dr. Wood and God on your side why worry. She laugh and I heard Dr. Wood laugh and say put her out. When I woke he was there to tell me everything was great and I could see my family then go to sleep the nurse would be here with me all the time. The girls came in and Sally told me what he just did, they asked if I really said that in the operating room and I said yes it was true. Then the nurse had them leave and I went to sleep.

When I woke I was in my room the nurse ask who I felt, did I need something for pain I told her all I needed was water. She said only ice for a while then water. Okay just something for my mouth. Next I remember a young man named Alan talking and a nice lady named Dena. He was a P.A and she worked for the hospital but helped the doctors. They were the ones that would be looking in on me. I had a few problems but not bad so I was sent home. I had home care in 7 days a week to clean and change the bandage. About the 5th. Day I asked the nurse if she smelled an odor she said no, then I asked what was this coming out of the bottom of the wound. She said don't worry I was fine. The next day a new nurse came she said I had a fever and looked at the wound. Right away she called my doctor and said he needed to see me now or I was to go to the hospital. I was told to go right over. Ray wasn't here so I called Carol she came right over.

When I arrived I was put right in a room, Alan came in and said let's take a look. He looked and said I'll be right back. In came Dr. Wood and Alan he started telling Alan what he was going to need and then told me that I had a bad infection and why didn't I call him before this. I told him the nurse said it was ok and had Carol give him my reports. I said a new nurse came today and called him. Alan came back and Dr. Wood looked at me and said this will hurt but has to be done now. I could feel him cutting but no pain when he opened the wound all kinds of stuff went flying. It was on both of them, me and the wall. Wood was very upset, he was with me for almost an hour before he had it cleaned out. Then he said I had to go to the wound care center at the hospital to have a wound vac put on. Since he had to reopen the wound he had to let it heal from the inside out and the vac would help. Carol took me there and Dena met us at the door. She helped take off my blooded clothes and put on a gown, then cleaned my up some more. The nurses were putting on the vac when Alan came in with my folder I could hear him tell Dena that Wood was hot and really yelled at the home care office. That nurse was not to see me again. By the time I got home Carol helped me to bed she had called Sally, I took a pain pill and went to sleep.

Sally woke me around 9 to make me eat some soup, gave me my pills and I went back to sleep for the night. Ray woke me to say he was leaving for work and Sally was making some thing for me to eat. He left. Later in came Sally eggs and toast and a hot cup of coffee. She stayed because the nurse was to be there at 10 and if it was the old one she wasn't coming in the house. Thank God it was the one that found it infection. She said she would be with me every day. There really wasn't much coming out but in a few days I could see that the wound was getting smaller. So far so good. After 2 months the vac came off and we just had a small wound to care for. I could clean it myself but the nurse still came 3 times a week till it closed. By the middle of August I was doing great I felt good and was hoping that Dr. Wood would let me go back to work.

One morning I get up and was glad it was the day for my appointment. For some reason I was having a hard time breathing so when I get to the office I told the nurse and doc sent me for an x-ray. My left lung was full and I needed it drained. I was sent down stairs to have it done and met a nice man Chris. He was nice and talked me through it. At the end he even gave me a hug. Very sweet guy. Went back upstairs and Dr. Wood said I had to wait three weeks to see about work fine see you then. I was hoping all this was over until a week late Ray came into my room and said he wasn't feeling feel. I looked at him made him lay down took his blood pressure and said we're going to the hospital. I told them he was having a heart attack and he was put in a room. They called his doctor since he was at the hospital he came and said he was calling a specialist in and have him look at Ray. I asked for Dr. Wood but he was on vacation and wouldn't be back till Monday this was Friday so one of his partners would see Ray. Ray was put in CCU and we were told that he was going down for tests. And the doctor would see us in the morning. While he was down stairs I called Sally and then his son Jim, Told him I would let him know tomorrow after seeing the doctor. Sally came and we went to eat I sent her home to get me warm clothes and a blanket I would be staying with him till he felt better. Then I went to the waiting room till he was back. The nurse called be back as soon as he was in bed. She told me his EKG was better and if I wanted to go home they would call if I was needed, with that he started yelling you promised to stay with me so I did.

The next day I waited for this new doctor but he was in surgery and would be for a few hours so I went to eat. Told Ray I wouldn't leave the hospital and they would call me if he came in sooner. Called Sally that the doctor would be in around 10 and I would call then. When I returned he was eating some eggs and toast, no coffee but apple juice. Around 10 Dr. Laron came in I wasn't sure I cared for him, he didn't look at you when he talked was looking into space. He said he was waiting to see Ray's stress test from Dr. Paul's office. More tests were needed and then we would talk on Monday. As he was leaving I stepped in to the hall and asked if I should have his son come down. He said yes. Ray asked what I wanted, I just wanted to know why we had to wait till Monday. Because no one was in the office on Saturdays he was okay with that. They came and he went down for more tests. I told the nurse I was going for lunch.

When I got down stairs I ran into Sally so we had lunch together. I called Jim and him and Barbara would be here tomorrow. Asked if he needed to be picked, no they would get a car. I said they could stay at my house. They would call Sally from the airport. Sally was going to my house and clean and change sheets for them. We went back to CCU and had to wait for Ray. Sally wanted me to go home and sleep I said when they get here I will. After he came back he and Sally talked a bit then she left. I told him the Jim and Barbara we coming he wanted to know why. I said you know your son try and tell him no. That stopped him from being mad. That night we had dinner together and talked. I told him I wasn't sure I like this doctor what's his name and was going to see if Dr. Wood would take over. He didn't care.

Around two am has I was looking into I hall I could see Dr. Laron coming in. I was hoping nothing went wrong with the tests. He sat at the small desk were the chart was and I went out and asked what was wrong. Nothing he couldn't sleep and had to check something now. Told him his wife mustn't like him leaving in the middle of the night, not married. Well your girlfriend, don't have one. I was hitting a brick wall. When he closed the chart he asked why I was here, said Ray didn't like hospitals and if I left he would too. We started talking about his family and his partners. He told me about a sister and brother that lived with his folks. After we talked about 45 minutes I said I would leave him to his work and went back in the room. He sat there for a few minutes then left. I was just starting to fall asleep when Ray said I like him, he is my doctor. I don't want anyone else. I said it was his choice and I would go along with it. Then we went to sleep.

After Jim and Barbara arrived on Monday we asked for the doctor. He was in surgery and would be in when he could. I left them to set with dad and I went to get some air. I knew I had an hour and it was nice just to sit outside and cry all by myself. A few minutes after I get back in the doctor had the nurse ask us to meet him in the hall? He told us there was no way Ray passed his stress test three weeks ago, that this report was wrong or not his. Ray's heart was in bad shape and he needed surgery as soon as we could get it set. Told him we needed to talk with Ray and I would have the nurse let him know soon. We went in and talked with Ray at first he said no, but we talked and he finally said ok. I told the nurse and asked the kids if I could go home and shower and sleep for a few hours to call the house phone when they were ready to leave and I would be right back. I left at 10 and they called at 6 so I did feel better. Jim said he would be back around 12 and I could go home for the night.

I was glad I had put on warmer clothes because he didn't come back till 8 and the doctor was already there. I told them Dad was going in tomorrow at 7 and he didn't know how long it would take. They stayed and I went home to bed. By 10 I was in bed and didn't get up till 5:30 called the nurse's station to see how Ray was and he was fine asked her to tell the kids I would be there soon. I took the spaghetti sauce out of the freezer that morning so I fixed the noodles and left for the hospital. Told Barbara salad was ready and all she had to do was heat dinner up. They said they would be back by 6 in the morning and if they took him early I was to call. When they left our pastor came in. So we talked and then Ray asked if I would go to the waiting room he wanted to talk with Jeff. Sure I went and had coffee till Jeff came out. We sat and prayed then he said to call tonight if I needed him.

When I went back he was sleeping. Good he needed his sleep. So I pushed the recliner back took the pillow and blanket and started reading my book. I must have fall asleep because around 4 I heard Ray yelling for me. I jumped up and went to the bed he thought I left him so I moved the chair next to the bed and he went back to sleep. I was awake now so I sat there, one of the nurses gave me a cup of coffee. At 5:30 the kids were here and soon they came to get him, we said see you soon and I kissed him telling him you did this once you will do it again. We were to go eat then stay in this waiting room.

It seemed like days but every few hours they would call to say things were going slow but fine.

Finally Dr. Laron called us into the hall. Ray had a stroke on the table and only have a quarter of a heart working that most of it was been going for a long time, I said he never said he didn't feel good till just this week. He said we could see him in a while but they would keep him in recovery till tomorrow. We were to go home and they would call if I was needed. He looked at me and said he will be sleeping all night so he won't know you're not here go home and rest you will need it. In the morning he will be going to ICU so take what was ours from the room, I already did. We saw him and he looked okay couldn't talk but I told him to rest we would see him when he woke up. Then we went home, Jim went for chicken Sally brought over food and I took a shower and went to bed. Didn't care if they stayed up all night.

Back at 9 doctor in surgery and would call when he would be in. The kids went to eat and I sat there. Kids came with oatmeal, toast and coffee. Dr. Laron came in and sat down. Ray was still out but that was find he needed to rest he was doing better and he was going to slow down some of the drugs so he could wake, he would be back later to see him. Great a few hours later they called and said he was up, we went back to see him he couldn't talk he had a breathing tube in so we talked to him. He went back to sleep so I sent the kids home then went and sat in his room. I was reading my book when the doctor came in he checked Ray out and said things were fine for now but there is no guarantee I understood. I was told to go home no one stays in ICU overnight and you can't come back in till 7 in the morning. There was no place to lay down in the waiting room so I left. The nurse had my number.

The next few days were up and down the kids had to get back home for work and that was fine. The doctor was able to get Ray to respond to his orders so he said in a day or two he would be going up to 4B. He was in his new room the day the kids had to leave so they were happy. Ray seemed to be coming along quiet well. But one day as I came on the floor I was told he was back in ICU so I went there. He was having problems. His kidneys won't work and even with the Cather he was having trouble. When Dr. Laron came in I told him that we both had living wills here at the hospital and what was I to do. He said it would be a few days before we would know what was happening. I said sir please don't lie to me with that he looked me straight in the eyes and said I don't lie about anything. I believed him. You could see the companion and caring in his eyes and face. He left the room. It took a few days but Ray was sent back upstairs. We were back and forth a few times. I was getting worn out I had my lung drained two more time they wanted me to have it telic but I said not while he is still ill. I can't be in one room and him another, what if something happened so Dr. Wood said he would have Dena keep an eye on me.

We were now in October and Ray was back in ICU. Sally and Carol were with me. I told Dr. Laron that I let them put in a feeding tube and wasn't supposed to, and he has been having kidney (dialers) for two weeks after his 30 days he doesn't know who we are and it's time. Dr. Larson looked at me and I could see the pain in his eyes, He said he would do what I wanted but would I please give him a week just one week to try something new. If it didn't work he would tell me. You don't live with someone for 30 years and don't have some kind of feelings for them I didn't love him but I didn't hate him either so I said yes.

In 3 days he was back upstairs trying to talk and looking better. Dr. Laron had PT coming in twice a day. They would get him up walking with some kind of tall table. First just standing then a few steps to the door and back. By the third week doc. Said he was to go to rehab and would be home be Thanksgiving that was the best words I heard in two months. So the next morning he was sent to rehab. I went and got all kinds of loungers for him and shirts so he would be okay with rehab. Sunday was a day of rest, but Monday he would go to the kidney doctor's office and have this treatment he would be back by 2. When I got there they told me they just sent him to the hospital. I was to go there

God I prayed I didn't want this to happen I should have made them keep him in the hospital, they put him in a room and said he was resting I stayed that night with him. I knew the nurse's there and they helped me through the night. In the morning I was told he was in a coma and was going down for tests. I went home took a shower called Sally and Jim told them it didn't look good and I would call after seeing the doctor. I was back by 2 the doctor was there, but said I was to wait he had to see me. By looking at Ray I knew it was over for him and it was my fault. I let him down I should have stayed with him. All I could do is watch him die.

About 5 Dr. Laron called me out to the hall. Told me Ray wasn't going to wake, there wasn't anything more to do. I told him it was okay just be sure he had no pain that I know he did everything and more for Ray but it was time to let him go. He looked at me and he was looking so sad. I could see he was in pain for losing my husband. I told him thank you for what you have done but in was in God's hands not his or his fault. I watched him at the station and as he walked away his head was down and his shoulders was sagging I felt so sorry for him or any doctor that goes through this, and it wasn't up to him. I felt he was the best doctor in the world. I prayed for Ray and Dr. Laron they would both need God tonight. I called Jim and told him it was soon be over that his dad wouldn't make it through the night. I would call later.

Sally and her son came back I was in the hall the nurses were cleaning Ray and taking off the machines. Just the IV and monitor was left on. We went back in and I let Benny sit on the bed and talk to uncle Ray I took Sally to the window and told her our brother Mike was on the way so was the pastor I knew it wasn't going to be long by the monitor soon the beat was down to 25 a minute and I had her take Benny and leave. It was dropping fast and I didn't want Benny here when it happened. They left and I went to the head of the bed and kissed him told him it was okay his family was waiting for him and I was going to be okay Just reach for the light, with that he took his last breath and was gone. With that in came 4 people and I moved to the bottom of the bed. One looked at me and said he was gone. So I called Sally she was just leaving the parking garage did I want her to come back, no I was fine. I went and sat at the window till Mike and pastor arrived then we prayed, talked a little then we went to the nurse's station told her I would have him picked up in the morning I went home for the last time. In the morning I went to the funeral home paid for everything and then called Jim and his family. Told them he was being cremated and I would have a service later. I would let them know when if anyone wants to come we would make room at my house.

Call Dr. Wood's office and told them I was ready to get my lung done I was tired of the drains and needed rest. Two days later I was in the hospital and Dena got me taking care of. I was to go home and rest for a week then see Dr. Wood. He said I was still run down and come back the week after Christmas. That was fine. After Thanksgiving I call Jim and told him that the 3rd of December was the memorial service for their dad let me know who was coming. Barbara just had her double lung operation so I told him to stay with his wife she needed him now. After that he only called when he was drunk so I stop answering his calls wrote him a letter and told him not to call if he was drinking that he did what he had to do his wife came first. Never hear anything till one of the grandson's called to say Barbara passed away they didn't take. Sent card and flowers. I didn't go.

Saw Dr. Wood on December the 28th. Would be able started work 1st. of January 2007. I was so glad to be able to go back and start a new life.

My New Start in Life

The first of January I went back to work at Mike's. A lot of old friends were gone and we had a new Manager, Mr. Scott. He was very, very young and knew everything. I was still a cashier and there were a lot of very young people now working there. The manager was upset because the rate for the cashiers was to scam 15 items a minute, that's not bad but new and working with old machines isn't easy. When he came complying about it I tried to explain to him he didn't hire people that knew what to do and being new weren't that fast. Well I had 1 week to get them on target or he was going to start letting people go. We had a heated discussion over this and I left his office with him mad. I was working with this nice young mother and showing her how to hold items and bag as you go along. She was doing pretty well till the register quit. Here came Mr. Scott, he was yelling what did you do wrong, how did you broke this register. Before I could say a work the customer asked his name and said she was calling home office, he had no business yelling like that at anyone and the machine hasn't been working right for the last 3 weeks she has been coming. As manage he should know it. She turned to my cashier and told her if he keeps acting like this to come to the Family Dollar Store and she would have a job.

He went back in his office and called me in, he was going to write me up because I said I wouldn't tell the company that the customer was wrong and he didn't do anything wrong, I was to sign the write up for my file. I walked out the door and went back to work. We heard the door sham shut and the girl from the office came over and asked what was up, told her don't know just go do your job. 7:00 next morning I opened the store the night crew left and at 7:30 Mr. Scott and office crew came it. I was working with Mary when at 10:30 the district manager came in. He was in the office when I was called in. Mr. Alacard was the D.M. when I walked in he got up gave me a bear hug and looked at Scott saying this is who you're having trouble with. I just stood there and let him try and get out of it his self. Then he turned to me and asked what was going on and I told him. Plus we went out on the floor and he watched how our registers were working, I showed how bad the produces was marked and with so many new people the scam count was too high. Around 2 he left said he would get back to me next week.

Within a month Scott was gone we had new checkout lanes and registers put in. Mr. Henry was nice. He talked to everyone as they came to work would let them know what kind of job they were doing, and things were getting better. By the end of summer I was having a hard time with my leg, so Mr. Henry said it was time for me to see a doctor. Summer was over and things were slow going, now was the time before the holidays. He said he could see how bad they were swollen at the end of the day. Told him I would call after work that day. I called to see Dr. Wood, I was told that he and Dr. Mann were doing Robotic Surgery but that Dr. Laron would be able to see me next Thursday at 1, I knew him so I said ok. Told my boss I had to have Thursday off to see doctor he was pleased I did what he told me to do.

Went to see the doctor he sent me down stairs to have some tests, when I went back to his office first he told me I was fat and had to lose weight. Told him I know that and have been losing, I was 298 when Ray died and now 269. I was still trying but it was hard okay. That's good but your still fat and need to lose more keep at it. I hope he didn't think I was going to argue with him all I said was your right I will keep at it. He was sending me for more tests and told me that the artier was blocked and he was going to clean it or put in a stent. I was to be at the hospital on the 28th. Of October 2007 to have it done. Because of my weight I could have problems but he would take care and watch me. Well he was right I was out for 3 days and he had to go back in and try something else. When I woke that nice lady named Dena was there she told me what Dr. Laron's did and what happened I had no blood flowing to my foot and he went in and fixed it. He would be in later to see me try and rest. Love when they say that, you're in the hospital in bed what else are you going to do have a party. So I slept.

A few days later I was running a fever and he came in. My sister was there and when he looked at my leg it was red and not looking to good. Sally said Sherry didn't mom tell you her and I were allergic to staples, the doctor looked at me then her and called the nurse to get him a kit. After he took all the staples out he cleaned it and put a large bandage on it. He told me it was infected and I could be in trouble. He would have blood tests ran to see how badly and would let me know.

Well it got so bad he called a specialist in. Dr. Baffle was very nice he looked at all the tests and tried a few drugs. Finally they came to me and said I was very ill and there was only one drug that would take care of this infection, it was Penicillin and I was allergic to it. That is one drug that can kill me. But Dr. Baffle said it would be done in ICU and he would be there when it started and in the hospital till we knew I was going to be okay. When I got to ICU he was waiting, my sister and her boys were there. So was a crash cart and Dr. Laron was on call just in case. Dr. Baffle told me there were 15 tubes and each one had Penicillin in them I was to drink one every 15 minutes with a little water each tube had more and more in it till they were gone. If I had any pain or itching of any kind I was to tell the nurse that was to stay in my room with me. If all went okay I would go back to my room, but I was to be watched I would have a bag of Penicillin and fluids going and I could call him if I needed him. Dr. Laron called to check and wished me luck, I said I would see him tomorrow. It took 4 and a half hours for all of this to happen. The nurse call the doctors and said I was fine so he put on the full bag. It was very scarier but if it was time for me to die so be it. Next morning I went back to my room.

I had a wound Vac put on my leg to help pull out the infection and heal the wound. I don't know how much Penicillin I had or how long I was sick but it was a while. Finally I was able to start walking, I was not a happy person I was down and felt like no one cared. If you've been in the hospital for weeks' time goes so slow. There was a time I was sick and didn't care if I died. I even asked God to let me go, no one cared if I was here of not. I had no one in my life, was all alone and didn't care. I was so bad I cried most the day finally I said to God to take me home or give me a reason and someone to live for. I was almost asleep when the door opened I didn't hear a word he said but when he left all I could do is say no God not him please not him. He is way too young and I'm not good enough for him, he would never want to be my friend. Right now I didn't understand. But every day I would wait to see him in the halls or when he came to my room, I would listen for his voice. I cared deeply for him as a very dear friend but knew things wouldn't work.

Soon I was going home, I couldn't wait for my office visits. He said I wasn't able to return to work for a few months or never depending on how I was able to walk. I had to figure out a way to learn to walk I had no feeling in the bottom of my foot and he told me I would have to learn to live with it. So I had to have something to do. I went and volunteered at the hospital I really liked my job. I was walking all over wing B on 4 soon I was walking A and B wings. I was so proud sometimes the nurse's would have me go for supplies or blood. That was a lot of walking. I was starting to feel like a person again. But my feelings didn't change. I knew I had to do something about it so I went to see a shrink. I went out of town but I wouldn't say his name or what he did, I would never say any think that would hurt him, or hurt his job. I didn't get much help so I called a doctor I was seeing up there when I was having problems with Ray. Ann wasn't only my doctor she was my friend.

We talked on the phone three times a week and I told her everything, He was one hell of a good looking guy, him eyes shined and you could look in to them and see how much he cared about the people he helped. He was one of the few that took his oath to heart. He gave his best and more. He would go in and see his patients every day. That's how much he cares about people. He was the best thing that ever came into my life. I didn't know what to do. Told her I was come to a friend's wedding. Great I could stay with her and Roger her husband. We would have a lot of time to talk then. Told her I would bring a few pictures I had of him so she could see his smile. Two weeks later I would fly in on Wednesday and staying till Tuesday then come home. It would be good to see her after all this time.

Roger picked me up at the airport, he asked me if I knew that Ann had cancer and it wasn't good. No she never said. I always met her at her office this was the first time I was to her home. It was on a very quiet street. Loved her yard, I knew she loved flowers. I didn't know one from the other only that they were pretty. She was on the patio when we arrived. Roger made her a drink and I had ice tea. She was so thin and weak, I asked how long she has been this way. We talked till diner Roger made Pork Chops and we ate by the pool. This was June, she said she was hopping to made it till their 25 anniversary, I couldn't believe she was that bad. We sat out there till time for bed we talked about all the things Roger and she had done. After her husband died she met Roger he was the guy that took care of their pool after a year they fall in love and were married. Most people didn't think it would last she was in her fourth and he was 20 years younger. But August would be 25 years and they were very happy.

They had a 6 bedroom yacht in Cancun and have been back and forth to their place many times. They were going again in July for their anniversary then she had to be back by the 1st. of August to see the doctor. The next day while she was napping I asked Roger if it was a good idea to go to Cancun, that is what she wants that is what she gets. The next few days she and I would sit and talk about my troubles. I told her I can't tell how I feel really, I love him but not how she loves Roger. I was mixed up and not sure what to do, how do I go on. She told me I had to talk to him let him know how I felt age isn't the factor it is something that has to be felt. Saturday I went to the wedding and when I returned Roger said she wasn't feeling well so went to bed. He and I sat outside and talked for a while then I went to bed. The next day Ann wasn't very well but she wanted to talk. I should tell him let him see how much I cared for him. She made me promise I would do it before she died. The way things looked I couldn't say no. I flew home on July 16th and they left for Cancun. Ann owned a condo and apartment building there and they were on the market so they went to see the realty estate person to sign papers, then fly home on the 30th.

All went well for her, she sold both places and was back to see her doctor on the first. A few days later they had friends over to celebrate their 25th. Anniversary. She called and I told her that I called him and told him how I felt but felt it was all wrong. It didn't sound the way I was feeling. Yes I love him with all my heart and always will but not as a women loves a man not like her and Roger. That isn't how it came out I'm still so confused. She said she was tired and would call again in a few days. Two days later Roger called Ann was gone. She made it till her anniversary and a few days more. She died in his arms at home with her family and friends. Just the way she wanted. She was a very big part of my life and I still miss her very much. Roger said he would still be there for me if I needed him.

I sent him a letter saying I would have to look for a new doctor, it wasn't fair to him to still have to see me. He helped me find a new doctor and I left the hospital and went back to work at Mike's This time the new manager asked me if I would be able to manage receiving, all I could do is try. So I had to go to another store for training. While I was working in receiving I had a vender named Stan, he worked for a beer company. We became good friends. He would let me talk about my life and tell me what he thought. He really helped me a lot.

Two weeks later Roger called and I asked him to leave me along. That I was going with a nice guy named Sam and was happy, he told me I was lying and I wouldn't be happy with that cripple and I knew it. So I told him I was the one to lead my own live leave me alone please.

Stan was there for me when my little sister died, I was at work and leaving the next day for home. He came in and asked why I was crying I told him she was 4 years younger and I should go first. He took off his jacket put his arms around me and kissed the top of my head and said cry, cry till you feel better. I did, till his shirt was wet. Then we sat and we talked for about an hour. He gave me his phone number and said call me any time if you need to I will be here for you. He was always the one I could count on he was the one that helped me understand how I felt. I told him he was right because I felt the same for him as I did for doc. That I loved them both with all my heart and always will that both will always be in my heart and prays. I was sad the day he told me the company he worked for was going out of business and he would be going to work for his dad up north. He would be leaving in 2 weeks. Before he left I gave him his Christmas gift it was still a few months till Christmas but I had one for both him and doc. and wanted to be sure he got his. It was a gold cross pen with his name on it. He was surprised gave me a hug and a kiss. As he was leaving he stood by the door and said Sherry I love you and I said I love you to Stan.

Sam was going to see family about 400 miles away then to see a niece in Ill so I asked him will you marry me. Sam's family here didn't care about him and he had no were to go so he said okay fine you make the plans and we will when I get back. This was an out for everyone. We would be married in name only live as if we were in love and he would have a family, mine that would be here for him and they are. We were married November 3rd. Had a nice church wedding with about 75 friends and family. We had a very nice day and everyone was happy. I still wrote to doc, and Stan keeps calling me from time to time.

Then one day Stan called and said he had something on his head and the doctor said it was cancer. He was going into the hospital in a few days and a friend Miss Jane would keep me informed. I never prayed so much or so hard. While he was in the hospital she texted me all day to let me know how things were going. When he was out of surgery she let me know the doctor said he would be fine the cancer was gone. I cried myself to sleep. Two days later he called for a few minutes to say he was alright but had to rest. So Ms. Jane, Stan and I did a lot of texting for a couple of weeks. I was overjoyed when he said he was going back to work. I keep telling him I waiting for him to call and say he is getting married, but that may be a long time in the making. So all I ask every night is that God watch over the two men I love with all my heart keep them save and may His angels keep their loving arm around them always Amen.

After Sam and I were married I retired and was able to be home. Roger called he was going to be in town and would I meet him alone I told him no I was married and Sam and I wanted to be left alone. I was happy and didn't want him in my life. Go be happy with your new wife. I'm sure Ann would be happy for you so don't call any more. Let me get on with my life and find some peace of mind. We talked about Ann and he said he knew I wasn't happy but he would stay away from doc. and me. He said he would give his number to Wes if I needed him. Wes was Ann's brother he was to the one that introduced me to Ann. He was my pastor at the time I need help and I still cared about him. So for a year I didn't hear from Roger, then he called to say that Wes was killed in a hiking trip and he was sure I would like to know. I thanked him and said now they were both together again. Praise God.

Sam and I have been married three years when three weeks before our 3rd. Anniversary I found out I had stage 2 breast cancer. Since I knew it was in the family when I talked with Dr. Drew I told her we would take them both off I didn't want one this year and then back next for the same thing. She agreed so I went in on November 14th. And had it done. Dr. Fuggy put the implants in and I went home. When I went in for a checkup Dr. Fuggy said I had a bad infection and had to have the implants out, also I had to stay away from my cats for a month. I was very upset my cats are like my kids, I can't leave them. But Sam said he would take good care of them and I would be home soon. I went and stayed with my friend Marie, She just finished her chemo and I helped her now she was helping me. I still had my pick line in from my surgery so I was able to have my IV injections done at home with home care service. So for 14 days I had a nurse come over and do the IV. The first 2 weeks I was getting better but the doctor said I still needed 7 more injections. Okay we did that and I was doing fine. Went to see the Chemo doctor and I would be started 26 weeks chemo and maybe radiation after that.

Finally I was ready to go home, I couldn't wait to see me babies. They were mad at me I was gone so long. Peppy wouldn't let me near him and keep yelling at me. I went into my room and cried. I had to keep them out of my room and off my chest for a month to be sure I didn't get sick again. 6 weeks after I came home the doctor said I was fine. I was to start chemo in two days and I could play with my cats. I left my bedroom door open and before long Peppy was up by me. He always slept at my side and I would pet him tell him good night then we would go to sleep. That was the first night in weeks that I sleep good.

Wednesday I had my labs done and the next day I would get chemo. I was ready, I knew how it was for Marie and knew I would be able to handle it. I found out that each person is different. I was fine until I had the shot on Friday, by Saturday I felt like I was hit by a truck every part of my body hurt. I called the office and was told I was given a new drug and would feel better by Monday. It is a good thing that I have 3 weeks between treatments. Four times I have to do this then 18 weeks just chemo. Not sure I can do this but once you start you finish it. I knew that I'm not a quitter. I have one more of this treatments left and I can't wait for it to be over. I can handle the chemo so I will be happy when that is all I would have. Of course all my hair fall out one day my pillow had so much hair on it, and I had it in my mouth, so I called my friend that does hair and she came and shaved the rest off. Sam and I were on our way home from church to meet her and I was sitting there pull it out be the hand full. I put it in and zip lock bag to remember it by. When she saw the bag as full as it was she started laughing most women try and keep it in for as long as they can and I pulled it out. So she took pictures, before and after. I know it will come back. I have a pink hat, scarfs and turbans to wear it is going to be a long summer.

Right now my head get cold and I get headaches and it hurts. I hope the guy I know can keep his warm I knew the hospital isn't always warm and your body heat goes out the top of your head. I hope he keeps his head warm in this cold weather. After my chemo Dr. Fuggy and I will decide if we go for the implants again or not. Right now I'm not sure. At my age I don't care or need them. Right now all I can think about is taking care of myself, take it one day at a time. I need a few good people that will be here for me and let me know things will be okay. Stan was here 2 weeks ago he can in from New York, and we did a lot of talking

Every time I have a major operation I get sick and almost die. I'm praying for no more. I hope this was the last. I think I've paid for my sins and need to try and make a friend of him, I only hope that I will see doc. and be able to have a nice talk with him, you don't know what happens when you listen to others and let them run your life. Well now I have it back and would like to take the time to talk.

This my story as up to date as it can be. I do want to remind all women to be sure you have all you tests done every year, ask questions, read up on cancer. Teach your daughters. Good Luck and I hope some were in this book you found something you liked. I enjoyed writing it.

So May the good Lord watch over you and keep you in His safe arms.

God Bless.

Our lives go on

Here it was a nice spring day, the snow was gone, flowers were starting to come up and Valentines is in three days. I made plans to take Martha out for dinner. As I sat here looking up and down the street I was thinking of all the changes that has happened in the last forty two years.

Martha and I were married at eighteen, right after high school. She was going to stay with my folks and go to night school to be a nurse. I was going to Viet Num. Martha is going to help mom and dad with my two younger sisters. Ruth fifteen and Sara fourteen. Dad's health was not too good and I had two years to give to Uncle Sam.

The first year was a hard one, dad got sicker and passed away, Thank God he left good insurance. He was a lawyer for forty two years and good at it. Mom and Martha were able to keep things going. Martha still worked at the grocery store and went to school nights. The girls were doing fine in school and with helping mom around the house.

After eighteen months I was sent back state side, I had a bullet in my side and had to come state side to have it taking out. I was at Walter Reed Hospital for two months then sent to Kanas for three months then mustard out in Georgia near home. I moved in with mom and the family. Times were slow and with the GI Bill I could go the collage. Worked at the mill part time and five night's school. I wanted to be a lawyer like my dad and granddad. It was a family trade. With Martha's help and staying here things were working out fine.

After being home for three months Martha told me we were going to have a baby. We were both over twenty and it was time to start a family of our own. Mom was on top of the world. Martha was working in a doctor's office and Ruth was going with a very nice guy. Sara would be out of school in June and the baby would be here in August.

Well time goes on. Ruth married Glen and Sara married Larry, Martha and I had three more kids. Joseph after dad, Elizabeth after mom, Grace and then Raymond. The way time flies kids grow and move on. Last year mom passed away at eighty two. She enjoyed her grandkids every day. All eleven of them. Ray was the only one still home. Only four months of high school then off to college in the fall he is going to be a lawyer too. Ten more years and Martha and I will retire and go off to see the world. Everything was so right for us.

Valentine's Day the kids had a sweetheart dance at the school. I took Martha out to dinner we got home around ten and were in bed when there was a knock at the bedroom door, Ray asked if we could come to the kitchen he needed to talk to us. By the time we got there the coffee was ready and Ray didn't know what to say. So I said just start. He told us that Kathy was going to have a baby and it was his. She told him tonight and was going to tell her folks went he dropped her off, she didn't want him to come in with her. He said they were carful but something happened. Martha was crying so I asked what they were going to do. Ray said he was waiting for Kathy to call, a few minutes later the phone rang. Ray answered it and talked for a few minutes then said Kathy and her folks were coming over Sunday to talk this over. Told Martha there was nothing more to do so let's go back to bed.

Saturday Ray and I worked in the basement putting up shelves and cleaning up the basement for mom. Talked about what he wanted to do and told him we would stand beside him no matter what. He said he was up all night thinking, He wanted to marry Kathy. They have been together since he was eleven and she was ten. Started going steady at fourteen and she was the only girl he loved. He knew the baby was his and he would take care of it. Of course I told him they could stay here till they got on their feet. But he would have to go to school like I did and we would help them. He didn't see or talk to Kathy that night.

Ten O'clock Sunday morning the doorbell rang. I opened the door, Kathy and her parents, Keith and Joan were here and things didn't look good. You could tell Kathy had been crying all night she didn't look good at all. I told them to come into the dining room and called the others. Ray was beside his self when he saw Kathy, Keith started yelling how both kids were no good, and look what they done to their family reputations. Joan started yelling that they had to quit school and get married next week-end. That Kathy was not going to get rid of the baby and she couldn't stay at their home. Keith started in again and Martha is yelling that they will stay in school there was only three months let. Keith said he didn't care about school they were both no good and he wanted her out of his house. Ray jumped up and I had to stop him from hitting Keith, Joan was screaming, Martha and Kathy were crying so I had to shout at all of them to shut up and sit down. This isn't helping anyone.

Martha went to make coffee, Joan keep saying they had to get married now. She wasn't going to have her good name dragged in the mud because of two stupid kids. Keith keep saying he wanted her out of his house. I looked at Kathy and asked if she had any idea how far along she was, she said she didn't remember if she missed one or three periods, she wasn't sure. So then we have to get her to the doctors for a checkup. Joan said she can't go to any doctor in this town everyone would know. I said spring break is next week we can take her to Rockton, Martha will make her an appointment with a doctor she knows there. Joan keeps wanting them to quit school and get married, Martha says no Ray isn't quitting school. That set Joan off again. Finely I said we don't know for sure if she is pregnant or how far along she is.

So this is what we are going to do, Martha you call Dr. Brooks and get her in as so as you can, Kathy that day if things are as they seem you will get the blood tests at Brooks office he will hurry it along for me. Keith yelled I'm not taking off work for her Joan you can go. Joan said we would have to be back before two thirty because her garden club meets every day till the fair gets here in May. In the meantime Ray and Kathy will remain in school. No one knows anything for sure and that will give us time to work on things out. Keith said ok but they were only to see each other at school and no calls. They left at noon.

Needless to say the rest of the day Martha cleaned the windows, vacuumed all the floors made dinner washed the kitchen floor. By eight O' clock she was ready for bed. Ray stayed in his room excepted for dinner. The next week was hard on all of us. Ray and Kathy only talked at school. Ray came to me on Wednesday and asked to talk it was almost the end of February and they were to order their caps and gowns what should he do. I told him to order both his and Kathy's I would give him cash for both. They were still going to go to school. There was only three months and two day till graduation so let's take one day at a time. We left town at seven thirty Kathy's appointment was set for nine fifteen we were there at nine. Dr. Brooks was a good family doctor he took Kathy back and told Joan he would call us back when he was done. She was not happy. I told Joan if she made a scene I would leave her in Rockton so she shut up.

After he was done he called us into his office. Yes Kathy was pregnant, but only five or six weeks it was hard to tell at this stage. She was in good health and so was the baby. He would need to see her again in three weeks and would be able to have a date for us. He gave Kathy a slip that she was under his care and couldn't have gym for the rest of the year. He sent the kids down to the lab for blood work and said a friend of his Mary, worked at the court house and would help with the license. There was a three day wait after we got the license. After we received the blood work we went to see Mary. Joan called Keith and her and I signed the papers because they were both only seventeen. Made a date to see the judge at two on Friday. I took Ray for a ring and Martha and Joan took Kathy for a dress.

Left town at one and Joan was worry about her garden club. As I dropped her off I told her to tell Keith to be at our house for dinner on Thursday so we could take care of this. We took Kathy to our house to talk and see what she wanted to do. She said her dad was being mean to her and yelling all the time. She didn't know what to do. I told her I would take care of it in the mean time she was to state packing all her things so we could start moving her here.

Thursday when they came I could see that Kathy was having a bad day? We had dinner then sat and talked. I told everyone that Friday Martha, Ray, Kathy and I were going to Rockton to see the judge. Did they want to go with? I was told no and don't bring her back to their house. She wouldn't live there anymore. I asked if they were sure Keith said yes, there were a lot of boxes in the garage so she could get everything of hers out before Friday. I ask Kathy if she was packing yet and she said yes most of her things were ready. I told her that tomorrow I would stop be after work and pick up what she had. Were there any big things I would need help with she said no, well maybe she had a hope chest her granny gave her and she was hopping to bring it too. Keith said he would be sure to have it downstairs by tomorrow. Said I would be by with the truck about seven. Most of the boxes were in the garage so she would be ready. Keith said to bring Ray so he could help, that he was taking Joan out for dinner and wouldn't be back till ten.

Wednesday Kathy called me at work, said her dad wanted everything gone of hers. That she was to leave nothing, He wants the whole room empty everything gone. So I called Ray told him to take the truck over to her and start taking everything out of her bedroom. Everything. I called Joan and told her that Martha and Ray were on their way and we would have the room clean by Thursday. All I asked if they don't say anything to anyone about what is going on. Kathy would stay at our house and sleep in a different room till school was out. They were both going to graduate and get on with their lives. Everyone agreed. Martha and Ray helped her Wed and Thur. then Thurs. night we went back for the rocker and hope chest. Both nights they were out. When we left Kathy was with us. She cried all the way home. I keep thinking to myself how can parents be like this, I would never do this to one of our kids.

What was going to happen when the baby got here would they be like this? Well it isn't up to me only time will tell.

I called Joan Friday morning just to be sure she didn't want to go, she said no and hung up. Kathy took her shower then Martha helped her dress. Ray and I were waiting downstairs as they came into the room. Kathy was beautiful she had on a light yellow dress and white gloves. Martha made her a small yellow veil that she would put on at the court house.

Got to the court house at one twenty. So we stopped and bought her some flowers. At twenty minutes to two they went to the ladies room and at five minutes to two they returned. Kathy had on the veil and Martha put some of the Daisies in her hair. She made a lovely bride. I took pictures of them they looked so happy. We stood before the judge at two and he let us take all the pictures we wanted. Mary even came in to take pictures of all of us together. It was a wonderful day we thanked them and left.

As a surprise we booked two suites at the Tower Hotel and took the kids out for dinner then told them we were staying overnight. Martha had packed an overnight bag for Kathy. Told them we would meet in the restaurant at ten for breakfast then leave for home. We said good night and went to our rooms, not much of a honeymoon but it was better than nothing.

We were home by two and it was so nice to have things over with. Less than two months till graduation day. Things were going very well, our house was on a large lot and it was hard to see if someone was there or not. Two weeks before graduation something happened at school and the principle called me at work and asked to meet me at the café after work. Jeff and I are old golf buddies so we met at the lower nine hole. He told me that Kathy got sick at school and he called Joan. She told him to call Martha she would take care of it. She did. But now he wanted to know what was going on. I had to tell him the truth. He said he should expel them both from school, married kids didn't go to school what would the other kids think. I said so far no one knows and since there were only two weeks left no one will find out. Jeff said yes both were on the honor roll and very good kids, sometime we made mistakes. What about her parents? Told him they didn't want anything to do with them so they are staying with us in separate bedroom till after graduation. He would let them go. Then asked how parents can be like that he and Carol have a grandson that was born six months after his daughter was married last year.

The night of graduation we were all seated the house was full. Kathy's parents seats were two roll down from us, they were empty. Sue from Joan's garden club said it was so nice of us to help with Kathy since Keith and Joan had to leave town Joan's poor aunt took a turn for the worse and they wouldn't be back for two weeks. It was so sad they would miss this day so she was going to take lots of picture for them. All I said was make sure you take plenty. Both Ray and Kathy were in the 4.0 group that was a plus for collage. After it was over we met up with the kids for dinner, everyone was telling Kathy how pretty she was in that yellow dress. Sue took a lot of pictures of the kids and said she would be sure to have copy's made for her family.

It took a while for Kathy to start to showing she was going into her sixth month by that time. When Joan can back from her poor aunt's bedside she told everyone that the kids ran off and get married while they were gone. That is fine no one is the wiser and no one cares. As for now Ray has a part time job at my office and will be starting night school next week. Kathy is in night school now hopping to be a secretary in an office. Both will have a good job and will be able to take care of a family. We will always be here to help when needed. Rays brother and sisters are so happy for them, the girls are filling the house with all kinds of baby stuff. I guess here we go again.

Peppy and I

As I was out for my daily stroll down our peaceful country road, I saw a box laying there no bigger than a childes shoe. I could hear a low meow, I picked up the box and to my surprise a little black and white kitten was inside. The poor thing couldn't be more than three weeks old. How could someone do this to the poor helpless thing, put it in a box and leave it here on the road.

He looked so sick and ready to die so off to the vet went kitty and I. After two shots the doctor said to call her in the morning if he was still alive. All we could do was pray and leave it to the man upstairs. I took him home fixed him some warm milk and made him a little bed for the night. I asked God to watch over him and went to bed.

In the morning when I rose he was no were in sight. I looked all over the house, at last I found him sleeping in my shoe by the bed. I guess he didn't want to sleep alone. Soon he woke up and was looking for food so I called the vet to ask what I should do now. She said I was right he was three weeks old so put him on can milk like a baby and bring him in two weeks. We will start him on food later but for now he is still two young.

He was so fired up running all over the house, I knew I had to give him a name. So as I watched him running I told him that I wish I was as peppy as he was. Peppy, yes that was a good name. Weeks passed to months and soon it was a year. My sweet little man was part of my life. For the past year I haven't felt all alone. As I lay on the bed watching him playing with his new toys I think of all the fun we have had, it was a lucky day for both of us when we found each other. Now he is the love of my life, my little man.

Each night before bed we play for a bit and he will lay on my chest and rub his nose on mine as if to say I love you good night, then he will curl up by my side and go to sleep. I would just watch him for a few minutes and thank God for him finish my prayers then turn off the light

As I leave for work each day he will walk me to the door, at night as I pull in to the drive I can see him in the window. By the time I get to the door he is sitting there waiting for me. I would pick him up and cuddle with him as we would go into the kitchen for his dinner. One nice thing he never complained about his food so who could ask for more.

One day I was hurt at work and had to go to the hospital, I had to stay for a week. My friend would go every day and stay with him for an hour but he was not happy at all. She said he wasn't eating very much so I called the vet, don't worry he will eat when he gets hungry. That didn't make me feel any better. I told the doctor I had to get home I would be able to take it easy and my cat needed me. He said one more day then okay.

The day I came home all Peppy did was yell at me, yes cats can yell. He wasn't going to let me forget I left him alone for so long. He even stayed away from me so I couldn't touch him. So I went and laid on the bed and here he came, he just wanted to be loved. For the next few weeks he followed me every were I went even to the bathroom. He would sit outside the shower to be sure I didn't disappear on him.

I went to see the doctor and he said he sent a letter to the company I worked for and told them I could only work four hours a day. If they had something I could do to let him know and he would let me return to work. So far he hadn't heard back from them and since I was receiving pay from them he wasn't going to release me. So I went home. That was Monday.

Friday doc. called he said to come in on Monday and he would give me a letter for my attorney and for work. I could go back but if I had trouble to call him. I dropped the letter off at the lawyers and went to the office to give them theirs. New manager, Mr. Albright. He wasn't happy I had to come back to work but main office said I did. I know they are just waiting to see what my lawyer was going to do.

Wednesday I returned to work. I was put in a small office and given some accounting sheets, I had to put them into the computer. I worked four hours and inputted over fifty accounts and balanced each of them. I worked ten to two. At two I asked when I was to work again and was told Mr. Albright would give me a call. Okay see you later. I went home and my little man was waiting for me.

While we ate I was telling him about my job. It was a piece of cake. This was what I did at my old job up north. We went to take our nap when Mr. Albright called, I was to work every day but could I start at eight till eleven. Sure I will see him in the morning. Peppy wasn't too happy someone woke him up so soon, so we went outside on the porch. We had tunnels and toys all over, posts for him to climb while I sat and read my books.

A few months later I was asked if the doctor would let me work six hours, I had an appointment to see him next week

I would ask. Dr. Peck said it was okay as long as I was sitting and could get up and move around once in a while. Took my letter back to Mr. Albright and next day started at eight till two and two fifteen minutes brakes.

Peppy and I were doing fine, we had our time and soon I would be retiring from work. At first we both had a hard time getting used to it. He would still wake me for work at 6:30 Monday through Friday. I don't know how he knew the days but he did. The week-ends we would sleep in a few hours. He did seem happy I was home all-day with him, I was too. One day as we were out on the porch I was watching him, he wasn't playing as well as before. So I called the vet.

Took him in the next day. If he was sick I wanted him to get what he needed to get well. She said no he is just getting old. He was now fifteen and still fine for his age. But I should start bringing him in once a month so she can keep an eye on him. She took some blood tests and said she would call me the next day. So I took my little man and we went home. As we went to bed that night I asked God to please let him stay with me I don't know what I would do without him.

About noon the vet called, he was doing okay but would have to start getting a shot once a month. Bring him in and we'll get started. We went back that day. The shot would help with the pain and he would feel better. Every month we went for the shot he was very good with them but would yell at me all the way home. One day he just laid in him bed and wouldn't eat. Back to the vet, he was running a fever so she gave him a few shots and me his meds. Told me that if he gets sick to call right away.

He seem to bounce back and we would do our thing every day. We still did his shot he was starting to lose some weight not too much but some. One day after his shot we came home and I fixed his dinner, I knew something wasn't right. The doctor didn't say anything was wrong but I could feel it. As he was eating I sat there and cried, tomorrow he will be sixteen years old.

That morning he was up and running, like he knew today was special. He was going to get new toys. We ate then went out on the porch, he loves pulling the tissue out of the gift bags as much as his gifts. He was having so much fun I started thinking back to when we started doing this. I must have thousands of pictures of him. We had a very happy day.

At night he would sleep with his paw in my hand and in the morning wake me with a kiss on my nose, it is his way to say morning mom I love you. I just ask God every night to keep him safe, he is the only one that loves me and it will be very hard when he goes.

So for now we take one day at a time and pray he will be with me a long time. But for now it is just my little man Peppy and I.

The First Winter Snow

It was my first Thanksgiving in our new house; both families were coming at 2:00. You could smell the turkey baking and of apples cooking and I just finished with the fruit tray. My table was set; all I had left was the cranberries to cook. Mom gave me the recipe, they were dad's favorite. Berry pulled the extra chairs up from the basement and set them at the tables in the den. All the young ones will be eating in there. By 12:00 my apples were done on to the cranberries. Berry's mom called to see if I needed help, I said no but if she wanted to, come on over. That will give Berry something to do. The men sat to watch some parade mom wanted to see.

At 2:00 everyone was there. The ladies were putting the food out, first Berry said grace, and then cut the turkey. Mom's made the kids plates. Soon everyone had what they wanted so we ate. There was food everywhere if you went hungry it was your own fault. After the clean up the men watched TV and the women sat and planned the Christmas Dinner. It would be at my mom and dad's this year. Around 7'oclock everyone was ready to leave. It was so nice to have peace and quiet from all kids again. Soon we were sound asleep in a nice warm bed.

It was a nice crispy November morning as I sat drinking my coffee I watched the last of the leaves fall. The weatherman said we would have snow tonight or tomorrow. I have some shopping to do so I better get moving. The day went well, dinner was over and we were sitting by the fire with our glasses of wine, then we saw the first flakes of snow starting to fall. We watched as the soft flakes drifted down covering the area. The first of the year and it was beautiful.

We woke to a big beautiful blanket of crystal white snow covering the landscape. It was a wonderful site. Every tree and shrub was covered with this white mantel. I dressed and with camera in hand went out to take pictures of everything. It was so cold and crisp; I loved it I believe that the first snow of the year is the best no matter how much you get. We had 6 inches.

The next 2 days were nice and warm and the snow melted. I was sure we would have more before long. Berry and I had lots of Christmas shopping to do so now was a good time to make our list and get started. We bought the lights for outside and a Santa for the porch. Berry's dad and mine came and helped us put them up. It was starting to look like Christmas all around.

Had 10 days of cold but nice weather, I got most of our gifts home ready to wrap. We still needed something for his brother and sister but I need his help with that. I love the crispy nights we get nice and cozy under the quilt that Gram gave us. A sweet kiss good night then off to sleep side by side. Yes I love the winter night. We wake to 8 inches of snow. The temperature dropped 20 degrees. The snow plows were out so we shoveled the driveway and sidewalks. Then we went for lunch and finish our shopping.

As we were leaving the mall we saw that it had snowed pretty hard while we were inside. We had a hard time driving home. I was glad he was driving. We got stuck twice but finally reached home. It snowed all weekend, 21 inches in all. Shoveled the drive 4 times and again after the plow went by. Monday on his way home he stopped and picked up a large snow blower. Thank God because that night we had 9 more inches. Yes in 5 days we will have a white Christmas. As cold as it is this won't melt till May.

The only thing I don't like is the icy roads and sidewalks. Slipped and fell getting the mail, Berry started to laugh after he knew I wasn't hurt, only my pride. Then we ended up in a snowball fight. Forgot how much fun it used to be.

Christmas Day was here we were all at my mom's. We have a great time and everyone was happy with their gifts. Dinner was great, the salmon turned out just right. After we all helped clean up we made plans for the New Years. The club was having a dance so that is where we planned to go; soon we were all headed home.

As we sat by the fire we talked about our first married year, and what we would be doing in the years to come. We took down the stocking that hung on the mantel. Each had small little gifts for each other. In the toe of Berry's was a little stocking that said Baby's First Christmas on it. Yes next year there will be 3 sitting here looking at the first winter snow falling all around.

Three Little Words

As I sat here waiting to see the doctor, my mind went back to a week ago. I was in her office and Doctor Michael's just told me YOU HAVE CANCER. How, I had my yearly checkup in October that was just 10 months ago, something was wrong. Doctor Michaels told me she was going to send me for some tests and a biopsy before we would know what we were going to do. Here I am again waiting. This can't be happening to me. All my mammograms for the last 5 years have been clean. One of their machines was wrong.

The nurse put me in a room and a few minutes later Doc. came in. She pulled up a chair, took my hand and said you have advance 2nd stage cancer in your right breast and under your arm. I didn't know what to say, I just sat there looking at her. Then I started to cry why me, haven't I gone through enough. What more can I take God. After I stopped crying we talked. Doctor Michael's said there would be more tests then we will decide what the best route to take was.

I went home and called Aunt Barb to let her know, she is the only living aunt I have left. We did the "hi nice to hear from you how are things going?" Then I told her, she didn't say a word for a few minutes. Then, Kathy do you want me to come down there? I can come and stay with you till you know what is happening. I don't want you to be alone. I told her no not yet I just wanted her to tell all the girls so they would be sure to have their mammograms every year. I have 16 girl cousins and my two sisters died from cancer. No one said what kind of cancer so I'm going to have to check into that. Aunt Barb then told me that Pam had breast cancer 15 or 16 years ago and lost both of her breasts. Aunt Lori died from breast cancer she was never sick and didn't go see the doctor until she started having trouble breathing. That was when they found it and it was already in her lungs. Plus I had 3 or 4 cousins that have had operations for cancer. I asked why I was never told all this. Pam, Carol and Peggy all had cancer 15 or 16 years ago and you didn't talk about it then as you do now. Aunt Lori died almost 20 years ago and you lived 1700 miles away and didn't see her when she was sick. We talked for a few minutes and I told her I would call as soon as I knew what was going on. We said a prayer together then good bye.

Then I called Joe, he was my sister Pat's husband. I told him what was going on and asked more about Patty's cancer. The doctors can't say if it started in the breast but she had it there, lungs and brain. The only thing was that Pat didn't tell anyone till they rushed her to the hospital two days before she died. Joe said he didn't know till then, she didn't want anyone to feel sorry for her. Still to this day I cry when I think of her. She was my little sister, we knew Anita was dying from cancer hers started in her liver and was sage 3 before we knew it. Patty died March of 2011 and Anita April of 2012. Two of my baby sisters gone. At least I do know mom had heart troubles.

Then I called the rest of my sisters and brothers and told them all what I knew and that I would keep them updated as I go along. Yes I'm going to stay by myself, no I don't want anyone here till I need help. Yes I have a girlfriend that will be sure to keep them on top of things. Then I said I'd call them next week.

All the tests are over and I received a call to come in and see Doc. Michael's on Monday. So here I am waiting and that is the hardest part. I know I have cancer let's just get it over with. We had a good visit. Talked of my family and the ones that had it and who died. I'm the one that has to make the choice. She gave me a lot of books and papers to read, and we set a date to put my port in. I will have the Chemo and radiation. After I go to the classes we will set the date for surgery. One day at a time. I find myself feeling better about it I guess that is because some very good friends have prayed with and for me. I know that God wrote the book on my life before I was born. So it is all in His hands.

Well I finished my reading and my last class today. My best friend is sitting here with me as we wait for the doctor. Today we make the final choice. As we looked over all the tests and reports we talked about what I wanted, what was my choice? We talked about all the pro's and con's. The best route is to take both breasts off. So that is what we are going to do. Doctor Michael's is going to be gone for 10 days as soon as she is back we will set the date. That will give me time to put my affairs in order, change appointments, and cancel a week end trip out of town and call family up north. Mary will take care of my cats while I'm in the hospital and she will stay with me for a week after I get home.

Things are going fine; the girls moved our trip up to this week end so we are going to party. Leaving for the beach tomorrow after work. Told my boss I would be having the surgery in a week or two and would be off work for a month after the surgery but was hoping to still come back. He said my job will be there for me.

Had a great time at the beach, sun tanning, meeting guys and out for dinner. Got a great tan will be the last time in a bathing suit for a while. We went for long walks and found some very pretty sea shells. Planning on doing picture frames for work to remember this trip. I'm lucky to have so many good friends. We just have fun. Back to work tomorrow.

This last nine days went fast. I have to be ready at 3:30 am tomorrow. So glad it is almost over. Mary is taking me to the hospital and will be there to talk to the doctor when it is over. I will have to stay in for 2-4 days then go home. The doctor said that they send off the tissue to be tested and she will call me to let me know how it turns out. I will start my chemo in 3 weeks for 6 months and radiation for 36 days.

I'm not worried anymore just glad to get started and get it over with. I know I still have a ways to go but I have a lot going for me. GOD has a plan, my friends and family are here and praying for me. What will be will be? I know that when this is over I will hear These Three Little Words YOU'RE CANCER FREE.

So please tell every woman out there that anyone can and will come down with cancer. But it is up to you to stop it before it starts. See your doctor, have your tests and listen to others.

God bless and be with all of the woman in the world.

Without You

As I sat here waiting for time to pass, and looking at the stars in the night I started to think of all the good times we had together. Sometimes it is hard to go on, why did you have to leave me so soon. I somehow thought that we would grow old together with 3 kids and maybe 6 or 8 grandkids running around. Then one day all my hopes and dreams were gone. One knock at the door and the officer said you were killed in a shootout with a drunk. You were doing your job, and I should be proud.

March 3rd it was a sunny day when we laid you to rest. Officers from all over were there. Your mom and I sat there the best we could as one person after another told us how sorry they were. Finale the Pastor helped us to the car and we were safe and it was so quite. This was the first time we were alone since the night you died.

I went to mom's house for a few days. She was going to put the house up for sale and go back to Ohio with her sister. We had a lot to do getting things ready. We were so surprised when the first family that looked at the house took it. All this in six weeks. First you were gone now she is gone, and now I sit here all alone. Should I sell the cottage and move or finish fixing it up and stay, I just don't know.

Chief Davis's wife stopped by today to see if I wanted to talk. I was so happy to see her all I could do was sit and cry. She stayed for a few hours and we talked and by the time she left I felt so much better. She invited me to a meeting for people that lost loved ones and is picking me up next week. Also she has a few of the officers and families going to come and help fix some of the things we were working on.

We were doing great the painting was done and the guys had the patio done. As we started to grill I got sick and passed out. The next thing I know I woke up in the hospital. Alice and Sue were there. I was scared and not sure if I was going to be ok. Alice took my hand a look at me, Kathy did you know you're pregnant? What, I was shocked. Then the doctor came in and said that with all that has been going on he wasn't surprised that I didn't know. I ask how that you've gone 3 months and it had to be a mistake. No you are 14 weeks, three and a half months along. I was in good health and so was the baby I could go home and just rest a day or two.

The girls took me home and fixed some thing for me to eat and put me to bed. Alice asked if she should stay the night, I said no. I needed time to think. What was I going to do? In five and a half months I'm having a baby. A baby, I had no idea what to do first. What will your mother say, she told us to wait till the house was finished and you were stable in your job. Well I will have to call her tomorrow. Maybe I'll ask her if she would like to come for the week-end and help set the baby's room. Right now all I want is sleep. Tomorrow is soon enough to worry.

As I sat here drinking my juice and toast I called mom, I told her I was in the hospital and the doctor told me I was 14 weeks pregnant. She didn't say a word. Then I could hear her crying, I ask her why, she said she was so unhappy that I would go and do something like this with you just gone. I said mom I was two weeks along when Mark died. That we both didn't know and I was sorry for her if she was unhappy. God left me something that was part of you and if it is a boy I'm going to call him Mark she said she wouldn't allow it and hung up on me. I just sat there looking at the phone.

But the time I got to work most of the people knew about it. Everyone was happy and the ladies were making a list of things they had that they won't being using that I could have. Plus now their talking baby shower. I did ask them to give me a few days to get used to it. We would talk about it later.

Well I made my appointment to see Dr. Scott on Friday. He said I was doing fine; that I'm 14 weeks along and that would be due September 12-15th more or less. We will know more after the ultrasound and if I wanted to know the sex he will be able to tell me at that time. I'm not sure if I want to know the sex of the baby, I want to wait to see when it gets here. In five months I'll know.

I stared to see that my waist was getting thick and would have to start looking for clothes, so some girls from work and I went shopping and found so many wonderful things. We even found things for the baby's room. I'm doing it in green and yellow, so boy or girl I'm good. We had a great day off just doing girl things. Things are getting better I even put a few pictures of you in the room. Our baby will know all about its daddy.

I tried to call your mother but she still won't talk to me, I asked the doctor to send her a report so she will know that this is your baby, her grandchild. I pray that you will work with God and let her understand we need her in our lives. I don't want her to miss out with our child. I will leave it in God's and your hands.

Alice is going with me to birthing classes as my couch. She said she will be there to help my on the big day. I'm starting to get the room in order. A lot of stuff was giving to me from ladies at work and the families at the police department. I put the rocking chair that was my mom's in there too. Things are starting to look up. I still miss you and wish you were here for all of this but I know in my heart you will always be watching over us.

Connie called me into her office after lunch. She wanted to know when I was going to be taking off for the baby. That business was getting slow and she was going to start letting some of the girls go. She didn't know if any would be coming back. I told her I was only 7 months along and still needed the insurance but if it was her choice then I would work it out. Connie said it would be in another month or so, she just wanted to know. I would want time after the baby gets here to be with it. That I would have 6 weeks leave once the baby was born so that will carry me through. I'm glad I put your insurance money up I will need it sooner than I had hoped.

It has been a hot summer so I spend all the time I can in the pool, Alice, Sue, Jeff and Ray come over on the week-ends and we put up a fence around the pool and a gate so as the baby gets older it will be safe. We are all still very good friends. Not sure what I would do without them. Sue and Ray told us they are having a baby in March, we are all happy for them.

Here it is August and I have 4 or 5 weeks to go, I was watching the baby move and kick for about an hour last night. I started to cry, wishing you were here to see this you would have laughed so hard. I will be working for three more weeks. The girls are having their shower next week-end. I will be all set can't think of a thing I need. I called my Aunt and thanked her for the gift card she sent; she said it was for dippers that I would need a lot of them. Told her I would send pictures as soon as I get them. She is coming down in November for Thanksgiving and will stay a few days that will be nice.

By September 5th. I started feeling like I was aching all over I had a hard time walking, sitting and standing. I called Alice and she came over, this is okay it is all part of it. We will be having a baby soon. We will make in till the baby is ready, just in case she will be here to spend the night and Sue will be here in the morning. I was so happy this was almost over.

Sue and I were having breakfast and the doorbell rang, I had a hard time standing up so Sue went to the door. As I looked up in walked your mother, she took my hands and started to cry saying she was so sorry and she wanted to be here with me when the baby was born. So now she will be staying with me till then.

We had a very nice visit and I was so glad she was here. She even liked the pool and the rest of the house. So glad I had all that help. September 10th I had my first pain as we were eating lunch. Mom took paper and pen wrote down the time and put it in her pocket. All day long she keeps taps on my pains. We went to bed at 10 and every two hours I was in pain and by the time we got up at 6 they was up to half an hour apart. Mom called the doctor with her report we are to call when 15 minutes apart and head for the hospital. I ate a light breakfast and went out by the pool; Alice, Sue and mom were all with me.

By then noon the pain was ever 15 minutes so off to the hospital we went. Met the doctor at the door and I was taken to a room. After I was ready the girls all came in. Soon I was having pain after pain so Alice and I were taking to the birthing room. I'm so glad Alice was with me, I was scared and I a lot of pain, around 4:30 in came the doctor and said we were ready to bring this little one into the world. I had to do a lot of pushing but soon I heard a baby's cry, the doctor looked at me and said you have a beautiful little girl then laid her on my chest. She was all pink and a strong set of lungs. The nurse took her to clean up and the doctor finished with me. I was sent back to my room and the girls were there. In came the nurse with my baby.

We all looked at her and counted fingers and toes. I looked at mom and said I guess we can't call her Mark so now what? We all came up with names then mom asked if we could call her Margaret after her great grandmother. Then we can call her Maggie. So little Margaret Janice Stuart was named. Mark I know you are here with us today and see our gift to the world. I know you will be watching over us till we meet you again. Thank you my love for our little girl I will be sure to tell her all about you. I will love you always.

www.ingramcontent.com/pod-product-compliance
Lightning Source LLC
Chambersburg PA
CBHW072017110526
44592CB00012B/1340